On a Wing and a Prayer
Faithful Leadership
in the 21st Century

LUTHERAN
VOICES

On a Wing and a Prayer
Faithful Leadership in the 21st Century

Michael L. Cooper-White

Augsburg Fortress
Minneapolis

OTHER LUTHERAN VOICES TITLES

Large-quantity purchases or custom editions of these books are available at a discount from the publisher. For more information, contact the sales department at Augsburg Fortress, Publishers, 1-800-328-4648, or write to: Sales Director, Augsburg Fortress, Publishers, P.O. Box 1209, Minneapolis, MN 55440-1209.

See www.lutheranvoices.com

Dedicated to

Pamela, Aaron, Adam, and Macrina,
the wind above my wings . . .

ON A WING AND A PRAYER
Faithful Leadership in the 21st Century

Direct Scripture quotations are from New Revised Standard Version Bible, copyright © 1989 Division of Christian Education of the National Council of the Churches of Christ in the United States of America. Used by permission.

Editor: Scott Tunseth

Cover Design: Koechel Peterson and Associates, Inc., Minneapolis, MN
            www.koechelpeterson.com

Cover photo: Koechel Peterson and Associates, Inc.
Author photo: John Spangler

ISBN 0-8066-4992-5

The paper used in this publication meets the minimum requirements of American National Standard for Information Sciences—Permanence of Paper for Printed Library Materials, ANSI Z329.48-1984.

Manufactured in the U.S.A.

07   06   05   04   03   2   3   4   5   6   7   8   9   10

Contents

Preface

The year 2003 marks the centennial of powered flight. Throughout this year, there are a host of celebrations and observances of the amazing feat wrought by Orville and Wilbur Wright near Kitty Hawk, North Carolina, on December 17, 1903. By the thousands, private pilots will wend their way in small aircraft to Kill Devil Hills airport, and visit the spot nearby where Orville flew the Wright Flyer for 12 seconds, piloting it slightly more than 120 feet over the dunes of the Outer Banks.

While some historians might argue the point, many who view the long sweep of history suggest that more than any other development or invention, powered flight has transformed the very nature of the world in which we live. Traveling coast-to-coast in a few hours, crossing oceans at will, hauling freight as well as human cargo at near the speed of sound—aviation has given humankind a radical degree of mobility in just one century. Air transport has revolutionized business and commerce, accelerated the pace of change, expanded tourism, and fostered globalization with all its blessings as well as its downsides for the human community. Aviation has taken us to the moon and made space travel seem almost routine, at least until the tragedies of *Challenger* and *Columbia*. As with any aspect of human invention and technology, the tools of aviation can be used for evil as well as for good purposes. In its most destructive manifestation, aviation has increased the ability to deliver a vast array of powerfully destructive weapons.

Among the valiant pioneers of aviation, especially those who fought in the skies during the first and second world wars, a saying became common: "I made it back home on a wing and a prayer." With their already somewhat unreliable aircraft severely damaged in dogfights or by antiaircraft artillery, it often seemed an impossibility that they would survive to fly again another day. Some of these heroes of the battles in the sky would nurse one crippled craft after another back to their home runways, or at least to safe landings in friendly territory. How did they do it? Many of these frightened flyers who lived to tell their stories testified to the power of fervent prayers. Entrusting their fate into God's hands gave them the courage to keep their cool under extreme duress.

While pilots flying modern aircraft in peacetime environments have far greater life expectancies than their pioneering predecessors, the world of aviation continues to require skill, discipline, planning, and occasionally a measure of derring-do. The domain of flight can be a great teacher, if one is open to learn its lessons.

Here at the beginning of the 21st century, leadership in any arena is challenging, complicated, and exercised in a complex, constantly changing environment. While day-to-day organizational leadership—in business and commerce, in government and community, or in the church and other nonprofit service sectors— normally is not a life-threatening venture akin to that of aviation's pioneers, it is demanding and stressful.

For more than a quarter century, the author has pondered questions of leadership. What makes good leaders tick? Are there really "born leaders," or can leadership be taught in some systematic ways, as is the case with science, languages, accounting, medicine, or other disciplines? Is leadership an inborn charisma or an acquired set of skills and mastery of processes and interpersonal dynamics? For leadership to occur, must there not be followers, and can "follower-ship" be taught, or does it just happen?

As I have pondered these questions, and reflected on my own calls to leadership in various ecclesiastical arenas, I have drawn insights from many sources—history, literature, current events, biographies about and autobiographies by great leaders, and many others. But the two primary sources for the metaphors and images that have been most helpful in my reflection upon leadership are the Scriptures and the world of aviation. As a Christian and a pastor of the Church, my personal and vocational identity is grounded in the Bible, the Word of God. As a pilot and occasional flight instructor, the principles and insights from the arena of my avocation also offer rich imagery for pondering how to lead, and how to convey insights regarding leadership to my students.

In this book, I will combine these two passions and sources— the Bible and aviation—in sharing my reflections on faithful leadership. Each chapter is framed by some aspect of the knowledge, tasks, and disciplines required of every pilot, whether s/he flies a tiny craft like my 1967 Cessna 150, or captains a brand new 747 for a transcontinental air carrier. Revelations from the great figures of the Bible are intertwined with aviation analogies and reflections upon my personal experience or that of others. My hope is that you, the reader, while not necessarily sharing my passion for the world of aviation, will be intrigued to seek your own metaphors by which to prayerfully ponder what it means to be a faithful leader. Most will be able to draw from experiences as a passenger in modern airliners where you may occasionally wonder about what's really going on up there on the flight deck.

A host of books and articles on leadership tend to focus on the personal attributes and qualities of effective leaders. My intent in this little volume is to give primary attention to some practical disciplines and conceptual approaches to leadership that readers might try out in their own settings. In so doing, I am keenly aware of how my own "social location" limits my perspectives. As a male member of the dominant racial-cultural group in this society, I enjoy certain privileges not afforded to women, people of color, and those of limited economic means. My social location limits my ability to observe and understand the richly diverse forms of leadership exercised by sisters and brothers whose life experiences and cultural contexts are different from my own.

An inherent liability in using the aviation framework is its tendency to convey the notion that leadership is a matter of mechanistic "command and control." As a Christian, I believe that ultimately we live by God's grace, not by exerting our will or by being in control of our own destinies. In the complex arena of human relationships where leadership of any sort is exercised, so many interacting dynamics elude easy description and can only be grasped intuitively. Servant leadership happens not as a result of taking control, but of letting go of personal agendas, listening to the hopes, fears, and dreams of others, and facilitating conversations as a group strives for consensus and common purpose. It is hoped that if the reader finds the flying analogies unhelpful or too mechanistic and culturally bound, you will do the necessary "translation" to metaphors that work for you in your setting.

If you're inclined to read on, climb aboard. Buckle up and prepare for takeoff. But first, utter a prayer and trust the old aviator's adage that "God is my copilot!"

Acknowledgments

So many people have contributed to the formulation of ideas presented in this book that any list of names would be unbearably long and inevitably incomplete. Classroom teachers, pastors and lay leaders in congregations, local community and national and international political leaders have all shaped my thoughts on this elusive topic of leadership. I am grateful to so many who have modeled faithful leadership for me—my parents, those mentors under whom I have served as associate or "copilot," Jerry Ramsdell, Stanley Olson, Lyle Miller, Herbert Chilstrom, and George Anderson. For nearly seven years it was my privilege to serve as chief staff person for a wonderful group of leaders, the Conference of Bishops of the Evangelical Lutheran Church in America. Most importantly, these ideas have crystallized during the past couple of years here at Gettysburg Seminary, where I am daily given insights about leadership from my faculty and staff colleagues, and from our students. In the latter regard, I express appreciation to the students who have shared their insights the past two years in a class on leading small groups and faith communities, "The Congregational System." My coinstructor, Norma Wood, has been a most engaging conversation partner both in the classroom and in our teamwork of leading this historic institution as president and dean. That I have the privilege to serve at this place is due to the good graces of the Gettysburg Seminary Board of Directors, for whom I am profoundly grateful.

I am grateful to Scott Tunseth of Augsburg Fortress for his faith in the project and his careful editorial work. Special thanks are due to John Spangler and Aaron Cooper for their review of the manuscript and many helpful suggestions for its improvement. Above all others, I'm grateful for Pamela Cooper-White, my spouse and favorite conversation partner, from whom I learn daily about many matters, including leadership. She too has offered insights that are reflected in the final product. The love, support, and encouragement from her and our family inspire and sustain me, and so the book is dedicated to them.

Michael L. Cooper-White
Lutheran Theological Seminary at Gettysburg

1

It's the Wind above the Wings

In a popular song recorded by Bette Midler and other artists, the refrain echoes over and over, "You are the wind beneath my wings." Undoubtedly, millions of dollars have been made from this musical piece which expresses lovely sentiments about a supportive friend or partner. Unfortunately, however, the song is aerodynamically incorrect, or at least incomplete. More than the wind beneath the wings, it's actually the wind flowing *above* the wing of any craft or creature that creates lift and causes it to fly.

Way back in the 18th century, a Swiss mathematician named Daniel Bernoulli discovered the basic principle that governs fluids and gases in motion. A faster flowing stream has lower pressure than a comparable stream moving more slowly. As Orville and Wilbur Wright, two sons of a protestant minister, discovered while studying their model planes in a wind tunnel, a slight curvature on the top side of a wing causes the air above to move slightly faster than the air stream flowing straight beneath the wing. It is this slight interruption in the airflow caused by curvature on the leading (front) edge and upper surface of a wing that stands at the heart of aerodynamics.

My observation is that leadership in any arena occurs as the leader causes a series of modest redirections of the energy flow in a system or community. There are many, many definitions of leadership—some simple, others complex. At its rudimentary level, I believe that *leadership means enabling change to occur by influencing others to do things they otherwise would not do on their own.* As the leader stands in the airflow of another person or a group of individuals and creates a series of slight redirections of their energies and momentum, lift is created. The individuals and groups so influenced by the leader rise to higher levels of performance. They are lifted up to see their situation from a different vantage point, enabling problems previously thought insurmountable to be solved, helping visions considered unattainable to be realized.

How is the airflow redirected?

There are as many ways of exerting influence and leadership as there are leaders. No two of us do it quite the same. The same leader exerts her or his influence differently in varying situations. As the president of a seminary, I lead in ways quite different from how I carried out leadership as a parish pastor, a bishop's assistant, or as a denominational executive. A teacher who moves from teaching at an elementary school approaches pedagogy quite differently in a high school or college setting. Yet, there are a couple of general principles that may be applicable in most contexts:

1. *To redirect the energies, the leader must be in the airflow.* In other words, it takes hard work, persistence, and in most instances, relatively long-term presence in a situation to exert leadership. Leaders who attempt to stay aloof, out of the pressures of the flow of energies in an organization or system, generally will not have major lasting influence in positive directions.

2. *To have significant impact, the leader must be connected in an interdependent system.* An independent, unattached wing will generate lift for only a brief time before it spins out of control and flutters to a high-speed crash with the ground. So too, a leader, whether in business or commerce, public service, the military, or within a church or other faith-based organization, must be connected, attached to others and likely to a whole community engaged in redirecting energy

flows. Individuals who try to go it alone, believing that there is one leader rather than a leadership team, sooner or later do damage to themselves and their entire organization.

Every person who seeks to exert leadership must analyze and understand the "system" in which s/he operates, along with its currents and flows, and above all the people with their hopes and aspirations, their fears and anxieties. By joining with others in an ever-expanding web of interdependent relationships, an aspiring leader soon begins to notice small and subtle changes. The combination of hundreds and thousands of interrelated miniscule airflow redirections soon begins to lift the entire organization to a new place.

Stall avoidance: Not biting off too much

Upon hearing the word "stall," most persons unfamiliar with aircraft and aviation assume it refers to the engine stalling out and quitting. In actuality, a stall occurs and the aircraft begins either to settle downward gently or rapidly fall earthward when the wings stop generating lift. This happens when the pitch angle or angle of the wing relative to the onrushing airflow becomes too great. Generally, though not always, a stalling aircraft is in an unusual nose-high condition just before the stall occurs. This can happen on takeoff if an inattentive pilot pulls the nose too high. Close to the ground, the stall may be unrecoverable, resulting in a fiery, deadly crash. Fortunately, unintentional stalls are relatively rare and almost nonexistent in airlines with two-pilot crews, stall-warning alarms, and other preventive devices.

In a stall situation, the wing is in essence "taking too big a bite," causing a disruption in the smooth flow of air over the upper curved portion of the wing. When this interruption occurs, the wing loses its lift-generating capacity and stalls or begins to fall. Leaders who get into difficulty and either never establish or at some point lose their effectiveness, often do so because they attempt to take too big a bite, usually at an early and vulnerable stage of their leadership.

A new minister who had just graduated from a seminary presented at his first meeting with the church council a blueprint for how this 80-year-old congregation could get off the downward membership spiral it had experienced over the past two decades. This bright, energetic pastor went on to describe no fewer than six new programmatic ideas, then laid out his staff and committee reorganization plan, and capped his excited presentation with a rough sketch of how the church's sanctuary could be redesigned to accommodate his plans for a radically revised new contemporary worship service. In less than a year, driven by a flurry of complaints regarding their new minister, the church council reluctantly asked him to resign. This well-meaning, creative, visionary pastor had simply stalled shortly after takeoff. He bit off too big a bite. The congregation's airflow was disrupted to the degree it could no longer lift members' sights. Rather than being inspired to reach attainable goals, members were overwhelmed and stopped trying to expand their mission.

In the world of business, entire corporations stall and are forced into bankruptcy or go out of business because they take too big a bite and find themselves overwhelmed. Those of my generation can look back over the past three decades and name the major airlines that once flew the skies of our nation or the world, but are now only memories—Eastern, Western, Republic, People Express, Pacific Southwest, Pan American, Braniff, Frontier, Allegheny, and on and on. With air travel expanding year after year, why have all these air carriers gone out of existence? The reasons are complex, to be sure, but in many cases overextension and attempts to expand too rapidly created debt loads and operating deficits that were unsustainable. Many other examples can be cited of small businesses and giant corporations that, at critical points, tried to take too big a bite of the future and found themselves stalling and falling into extinction.

Flaps and other lift-enhancers

On a jetliner beginning the final phase of its landing approach, usually right about the time the passengers are instructed to return their seats and tray tables to the full upright position, one begins to hear a low grinding sound akin to a dentist's drill in slow motion. Passengers in window seats over the wing may notice big metal panels rolling out backward and downward from the rear or trailing edge of the wing. Up front, the captain or copilot has begun to lower the flaps, rather ingenious devices that both expand the surface of the wing and also increase its curvature. These two effects in combination increase the wing's lift, enabling the aircraft to fly at a lower speed and prepare for its touchdown. Sophisticated high-performance aircraft have some other lift-enhancers in addition to the flaps, including wingtips and high lift devices.

What are some lift-enhancing devices that leaders might extend to increase their effectiveness and enhance their leadership? Again, they are as many and varied as are leaders themselves. In general, continuing one's education and seeing it as a lifelong process will increase leadership ability. Honing one's communication skills through courses or disciplined self-study can be another lift-enhancer. Increasingly in a world made smaller by air travel and the marvels of modern media, learning and becoming fluent in another language will enable one to lead in an expanded arena of influence.

Many leaders in churches have found both inspiration and leadership enhancement by learning from the experiences, writings, and practical wisdom of faith-based community organizers. In my own case, working with such organizers in several settings and studying their methodologies, such as one-on-one interviews, issue-identification in diverse communities, and the development of practical, achievable goals that truly improve people's lives have been lift-generators for me.

While the addition of flaps to airplanes has enhanced the performance of wings, there is a downside to them as well. In addition to increasing lift, flaps also increase drag. There are limits to how big and how heavy a wing can be. Leaders too can become so weighed down with excess appendages that they lose their primary focus. The would-be teacher who forever remains a full-time student will never know the satisfaction of imparting knowledge and wisdom to other eager learners. The salesperson or executive who is forever running off to training conferences may be dragged down by too many days off the floor or out of the office. Every wing has a particular airspeed and configuration at which it generates maximum lift and minimum drag. So, too, a leader needs to discover her or his proper balance between sustaining ongoing efforts and taking time out to add lift-enhancing experiences and education.

Getting rid of ice and other lift-destroyers

Just as there are lift-enhancers like flaps and wingtips, so in the world of flight there are lift-destroyers. Chief among them is the slow or rapid accumulation of ice on the wings and other aircraft components. Especially for those of us who fly small and simple airplanes without the sophisticated ice prevention and removal equipment present on all airliners and other large aircraft, avoiding icing conditions is one of the highest priorities. Once it builds up, in a matter of minutes it can severely reduce or totally destroy the wing's lifting capacity, causing a stall that is usually unrecoverable.

Leaders too must seek to avoid those factors that can weigh us down and cause us to stall and begin a downward tailspin. What are some of those factors that are frequent lift-destroyers for leaders? Allowing inappropriate criticism to stick in one's craw can be as deadly as a heavy layer of ice on the wings. None of us who seek to lead should be above criticism or so hardened and rigid we cannot hear alternative points of view. But taking personally every petty criticism out there in the airflow around us is almost a guaranteed tailspin-inducer. So is giving too much attention to our own self-doubt and hesitancy in moving forward. Again, we who would lead should not be cocky or overly self-confident to the point of shutting out alternative visions and perspectives. But questioning every inclination, debating over and over again with coworkers the same minor points and procedural issues can have a chilling effect and lead to a stalling paralysis of leadership.

While some of the lift-destroyers are internal and self-induced, others are external and generated by the environment around us. Allowing boards of directors, church councils, and other governing groups to micromanage can be deadly for the would-be leader. For over a dozen years, I lived in the city of Oakland, California. A beautiful, richly diverse community with people of extraordinary gifts and talents, Oakland—like most cities—sadly witnessed an ongoing decline in the quality of its public schools. In my judgment, it was not that the Oakland public schools lacked good teachers and administrators or visionary top leaders. In fact, a series of superintendents were highly regarded nationwide by many of their peers. What then caused the growing dysfunction in the Oakland schools? In the judgment of many observers, a major contributor was the school board's tendency to intrude in management decisions. One after another, highly gifted superintendents left their post after a brief tenure. They simply could not be effective in an atmosphere where their board bosses were second-guessing every decision, getting involved in hiring and firing of administrative personnel, visiting schools and seeking to direct the work of local principals and teachers, and engaging in other destructive behaviors. What can the leader do if external forces keep sending freezing rain one's way? In addition to the deicing fluid sprayed in inclement conditions just before takeoff, modern high performance aircraft have a variety of ice-shedding devices like in-wing heating devices, or rubber boots that expand like a balloon on the wing's edge to break off the ice. Propeller-driven aircraft likewise have deicing devices that keep them from ice buildups that can destroy their lift.

Effective leaders need to discover their individual ice-shedding devices and aids. For some, it may be regular consultation with a management expert or personal therapist. For others, some coaching in how to separate helpful, constructive criticism from general negativity and chronic complaining can be a helpful deicer. The regular pursuit of hobbies and avocations, vigorous physical exercise, and healthy friendships are also crucial to maintaining a well-balanced life. As a Christian, I believe that commitment to and participation in a community of God's faithful worshiping people is essential to maintaining a healthy spiritual life and mitigating the destructive effects of all the forces of sin and evil.

There's lift going downward too

In our common usage, "lift" connotes going upward, being raised higher. But the wings of an aircraft descending to land are still generating lift. The airfoil which constitutes the portion of an aircraft's tail section called the horizontal stabilizer is shaped so that lift is always generated in a downward direction. Without this balancing effect of the "tail feathers" which generate lift opposite to that of the wings, the nose would soon point straight downward and all the plane's occupants would be doomed.

In general, society seems to regard as dynamic leaders those who are taking their organizations to new heights of success, climbing ever upward on the corporate ladder, and showing increasing profits in business or increased membership in church or other voluntary associations. But it's important to realize that lift and good leadership are often being exercised by those who find their organization moving in what may be viewed from some vantage points as a downward direction.

Many chapters of my ministry as a pastor in the Lutheran church have been spent in places where membership growth, financial expansion, and other outward signs of success eluded us. As a pastor at an inner-city congregation in a changing community, it was not my destiny to be written up in our denominational publication for a rapidly growing ministry success story. Nevertheless, lives were being touched by God's good news. People were growing in their faith, finding richly varied educational opportunities, and standing collectively as a beacon of hope in a depressed neighborhood. Lift was being generated as our financial resources continued on a slow downward spiral. Later, for a decade I served as director of an urban coalition of parishes, again with most in economically depressed, troubled, hurting communities. No mega-churches evolved out of those struggling outposts of ministry. But God's Word was being proclaimed, and one by one some young people were having doors opened and alternatives to otherwise bleak futures placed before them by these little churches. Some of those congregations no longer exist. But they went down generating lift until the last moment.

In the arenas of commerce, government, education, and others as well, there are similar seasons of decline when an organization is shrinking rather than growing. While the market for automobile tires expanded exponentially, there was a great downturn in business for blacksmiths installing horseshoes. Those whose skills were exclusively in typewriter repair find themselves passed by in the age of the computer. Often, those who lead an organization during its stormy downward cycle are no less creative or competent than past leaders who had the good fortune of piloting amidst sunny, tranquil skies.

Who are leaders?

All of us can point to great figures of history whose leadership has loomed large on the world's stage, either for good or for ill. Alexander the Great, Napoleon Bonaparte, Mahatma Gandhi, Adolf Hitler, Winston Churchill, Franklin Roosevelt, Indira Gandhi, Juan and Eva Peròn, Nelson Mandela—these and many other political leaders on the global scene have inspired both horrendous cruelty and courageous heroism on the part of millions of their followers. Each in turn cast a grand vision and enlisted or forced great masses of people to move to a new place in their work, philosophies, and commitments. Sadly, too often a demonic leader's vision included domination and even extermination of others. But ethical women and men down through history also prevailed in many instances when the future of a nation, or at least significant numbers of people, demanded heroic acts of leadership.

In our own time, the word "leader" evokes a broad range of images: international political figures, sports heroes, military commanders, successful entrepreneurs, local officials, or beloved persons who lead in community and church groups in every city, town, and village. Some careful reflection on the way each of these persons currently exercises a redirection of the airflow in their own lives and those of others can yield a rich education in the *how* of leadership.

A lift-generating colleague

When faced with the question, "Who are current leaders?" many of us will tend to mention those household names cited often in the national or international media. But we need not look so far away for strong, courageous, competent leaders. As I share my reflections on one leader "close to home," I invite you, the reader, to reflect on those within your own immediate circles of family, friends, coworkers, or neighbors who are truly strong, lift-generating leaders.

For the past five years, the seminary where I serve has been blessed with a lift-giving leader in the dean's office. Dr. Norma Wood has been around our institution in various capacities for over 30 years. She has worked in admissions, as counselor to students, as instructor, assistant, associate, and finally a full professor of pastoral counseling. As one of only a half dozen in its history to bear the title of dean, Dr. Wood is the first woman to hold that office.

As I think of leaders in the ways defined in this chapter, Norma's graceful adeptness at causing thousands upon thousands of small creative, lift-generating disruptions in the airflow of people's lives is exemplary. I observe it in her daily interactions with our students, staff, and faculty colleagues. An encouraging word, an easy-going "you can do it" attitude, a cheering e-mail in the morning, a reassuring smile for an anxious first-year student—these are the daily small interventions that lift so many to a little higher place.

Gentle and loving, my colleague can also be tough-minded and strong-hearted when the situation demands. For the sake of the larger community, individuals must sometimes be told a firm "no." Students failing their courses or acting inappropriately in their field education situations sometimes need a gentle reprimand. Some occasional serious disrupters of community life, or those who exhibit conduct unbecoming future ministers of the church, must face stronger disciplinary measures. Even in these extreme and rare situations, however, I have never observed my colleague as failing to find some words of encouragement, or leaving another person without hope for a brighter future. Quite simply, my friend and coworker reminds us all that we are beloved of God and destined as spiritual persons to inherit the coming reign of God.

Some biblical lift-makers

As I ponder the Scriptures, there are numerous examples of holy, yet very human, lift-generators. Inspired by God to go out on a journey to an unknown destination, Abraham and Sarah lifted their eyes to the Lord and believed in a promise. Their willingness to move out of their normal routines and familiar places must have caused significant disruptions of the airflow for others around them. Advanced in years, even as their lives were disrupted in major measure by God's promise of a son, they kept faith and became leaders in God's new movement that led to the formation of a people.

Or I think of the great wings extended into the winds of change by John the Baptist as he urgently and persistently encouraged others to prepare the way of the Lord. Not a flashy figure with an impressive pedigree at all, the Baptizer led by inserting himself into the daily lives of common folk going about their regular routines, calling them to turn and go in a new direction. In so doing, he caused some slight deviations in the airflow around him, and more than a few were opened to look with new eyes upon the one named Jesus who would soon follow in John's wake.

Our Lord himself, of course, was the great lift-giver who declared, "And I, when I am lifted up from the earth, will draw all people to myself" (John 12:32). In the early days of his ministry, before his fame as a miracle worker flourished, no one was asking for Jesus' intrusion into their lives. But time and again, in chance encounters along the road, in brief quiet conversations at the hearth or in his public teaching, Jesus caused thousands upon thousands of disruptions in the normal currents of people's lives. And in these redirections of the airflow of their lives, he directed his followers God-ward.

For reflection

1. Who are those individuals who have generated lift in your life? How did they do so?
2. What are the lift-destroyers in your workplace? In other arenas of your life?
3. As you think about deflecting the airflow in a particular setting, what are some concrete ways to begin?
4. Which other biblical leaders come to mind as you think of those who made a difference? How did they change the "airflow" in their situations?
5. Think about your congregation or place of work. Would you describe it as an organization that is on the rise, or descending? What kind of leadership "lift" is needed right now, and why?

2

Preflight Planning: The Key to Success

While "jump in and go" is the attitude most of us take with regard to our automobiles, it is not the approach flight instructors teach their budding pilots. Just the opposite is the case. From their first flight lesson, pilots are taught the critical importance of thorough preflight planning. Even if the day's objective is a brief scenic tour of the local area, always within sight of the departure airport, the ultimate success and safety of a flight hinges on a good preflight inspection and briefing.

Not only is preflight planning prudent; it is a legal requirement for all pilots under all conditions. The key Federal Aviation Regulation (FAR) is 91.103: "Each pilot in command shall, before beginning a flight, become familiar with all available information concerning that flight." Failure to comply, especially if such negligence contributes to an accident, can result in serious sanctions, and even constitute cause for both criminal prosecution and civil litigation.

Pilots are taught that allowing sufficient time for a preflight planning session is absolutely essential. A rushed flyer is likely to overlook something critical. A hurried pilot endangers self and passengers. Preflight planning includes several key dimensions: a careful examination of the aircraft itself and a determination of its proper loading, checking the weather and gathering information about the destination airport and its likely conditions at the time of arrival, determining fuel needed with ample reserves, and most importantly of all, self-examination regarding the pilot's own condition on the day of the planned flight.

So it is, I contend, for leaders in any setting. A cavalier "jump in and go" attitude usually isn't the most effective way to go. Careful forethought and planning are the keys to the success of a venture. Assessing a work group or faith community's resources, scanning the environment and examining all the contextual trends and realities that will affect the organization, setting clearly defined goals and objectives, and reviewing the leader's own capabilities and shortfalls all contribute to achieving desired outcomes.

Know your craft and your own condition

Few things make a flight instructor or seasoned pilot more nervous about fellow aviators than to see a hurried, harried pilot rush out to an airplane, unfasten its tie-down ropes or chains, kick a tire, jump in and fire up the engine for a rushed departure.

In contrast to this "kick and go" attitude, a safe and cautious pilot conducts a thorough walk-around of the airplane before loosening it from its moorings. Every visible portion of the aircraft gets a careful review by an experienced eye. During preflight, the prudent pilot checks fuel and oil levels and condition, eyeballs all the exterior flight control surfaces, examines ailerons, flaps, rudder and other moveable parts, opens the engine compartment cowling and scrutinizes for anything that seems amiss.

Continuing in the preflight process, especially if the airplane is an unfamiliar rental, the pilot reviews the POH or pilot's operating handbook, particularly noting key airspeeds, any unusual characteristics of the aircraft, and the checklist for emergency procedures. Every airworthy craft must have on board some current paperwork—legal registration, an airworthiness certificate, weight and balance information—in addition to the POH, so the pilot must determine that these documents are in fact within the aircraft. Reviewing the paperwork also includes careful scrutiny of the aircraft logbook and "squawk sheet," a notebook or clip board on which other pilots have squawked, that is, noted any discrepancies or deficiencies experienced on recent flights. While some such "squawks" are acceptable nuisances and do not ground the aircraft, others compromise safety and necessitate some repairs before the plane can again be taken aloft.

An effective leader in any arena likewise periodically takes a step back from day-to-day involvement in details to assess her or his organization, community, or enterprise. What is the overall condition of this organization and its many components? Do we have ample resources to fuel a proposed project or venture? If not, how can they be gathered and garnered in order to propel us to an important destination? Are there some broken or fragile parts that need attention or replacement before we can take off to envisioned new horizons?

In many ways, the most important aspect of a thorough preflight screening is the pilot's own self-examination. If the pilot is, after all, the most important "component" in a safe and airworthy flying machine, then her or his physical, mental, and spiritual condition merits close scrutiny. The process of self-examination includes a candid assessment of whether or not one is properly equipped and prepared for a particular task of leadership. With roughly 1,000 hours in a variety of single-engine aircraft, I can assure my passengers of their relative safety with this pastor/pilot at the controls of a typical Cessna or Piper. But put me in the left seat of a Boeing 747, and I'd strongly recommend that all the passengers run for the jet ways to escape their guaranteed demise! I'm simply not trained and equipped to fly complex turbine-powered multiengine aircraft.

Conversely, pilots of airliners and other large aircraft sometimes have difficulty transitioning to small aircraft. They become so accustomed to the sophisticated equipment and multiperson cockpit environment that they fail to transplant themselves into the more "seat of the pants" context of a lightweight little plane. While on a gate hold at San Francisco airport some years ago, the captain invited any interested passengers to come up to the cockpit for a visit. For a half hour or so I chatted with him and other crew members. He shared that when not flying the big birds, he piloted his own Cessna. It was important in so doing, he indicated, that his wife or someone else accompany him and remind him he needed to get lower to the runway before landing! In the 747 the cockpit is about 30 feet off the ground when it's on the ground. "You're a little high, aren't you dear?" his wife often reminds him, thus preventing a gear-crunching, drop-in landing in their Cessna.

On occasion, I have witnessed previously effective leaders quickly crash and burn in a new context. In many instances, they were "over their heads," having been promoted to a new position without the requisite skills and training required. In other situations, it was just a mismatch, and the leader was in a context or community where s/he was ill-equipped to serve.

Effective leaders who recognize the importance of self-examination exercise this discipline in a variety of different ways. Many leaders find they need significant periods of time alone to regroup, to ponder their own feelings, and to reflect, pray, and meditate. At least some of the time, most of us need the perspective of others to help us assess the state of our well-being. Regular medical checkups, periodic consultation with an objective professional consultant or therapist, the cultivation of deep friendships with persons who will tell us the truth even when it's hard to hear—these and other measures can be important aspects of assessing and stewarding one's own fitness.

Calculating weight and balance

Yet another aspect of preflight planning that is both practically important and legally required is the careful calculation required to determine that an airplane is within its overall weight limitations, and also that it is properly balanced for safe operation. I remember how my father could overload a so-called half-ton pickup with grain or gravel to the point the truck bed would collapse the rear springs and make for a very rough ride. While that made for an uncomfortable and unusually bumpy trip home or into town, the pickup's overloading did not seriously compromise life and limb. Not so in an airplane! Overloading beyond the allowable maximum gross weight, or improperly loading so as to cause an out-of-balance situation can have devastating effects. In the recent post-takeoff crash of a commuter airliner departing from Charlotte, North Carolina, preliminary post-accident speculation points toward the possibility that the aircraft was too heavy and had too much baggage in rearward compartments.

Leaders in any setting need to calculate the weight and balance within their organization. Do we have the proper mix of gifts and talents within our community or work group? If not, where might people be found who bring those gifts, and how can they be invited to join us? Are things in good balance? Do we have enough diversity, or are we overloaded with like-minded people who may be tilting us enough so that we're unwittingly flying in a big circle and not proceeding forward in our mission? Are we carrying too much baggage, unhelpful and possibly inaccurate reminiscences of a bygone golden era in our history? Are there a few noncontributing and unhelpful passive "passengers" who need to be coaxed to take another flight where they may be happier, enabling us to get on with our tasks unencumbered by this "dead weight"?

This kind of weight and balance assessment is especially critical with regard to an organization's top level management or board of directors. As vacant spots occur on our seminary board, for example, our board chairperson and other leaders join me in assessing our overall balance. While most of our board members are elected by supporting constituencies, we can make recommendations to nominators. A strong faith and spiritual commitment is a given in our search. But we go on to ask if we also may need persons who have financial, legal or fund-raising expertise. Do we have enough educators who understand the importance of a vibrant academic life, and who can ensure that our faculty receives strong support? How's our balance in terms of gender, racial diversity, and, in our case, also a mixture of clergy and lay leaders? Given that we see ourselves as a professional graduate school serving a national and even international constituency, what about our geographical spread on the board of directors?

From time to time, in many organizations or communities, the weight and balance assessment may cause leaders to conclude that some difficult decisions must be made. An employee who is unproductive over a prolonged period and merely occupying a position on the organizational chart may have to be let go. Or a volunteer whose attitudes and actions, while previously energizing and contributing to the overall mission, may now be dragging down a community's spirit. In such a situation, again after repeated efforts to help the person move to a different place where s/he and the overall community will be in better balance, an ultimate difficult decision to ask the person to transfer energies elsewhere may be in the best interests of the individual and all concerned.

Mission planning: Determining the destination

On a bright spring morning or a quiet autumn evening, I occasionally get my little two-passenger Cessna 150 out of its hangar at the local airport and do a thorough preflight as described above. Determining that the aircraft is in good shape, has ample clean fuel, is appropriately balanced and under its allowable gross weight, I wonder where I should go. Once in a while the only destination is to land back at Gettysburg after a peaceful aerial tour of the battlefield and local area.

Most times when I fly, however, I'm actually going somewhere out of the local area, and that requires some careful cross-country flight planning. It may be a weekend trip to Philadelphia where my spouse serves at another seminary, or a work-related trip somewhere in Pennsylvania or elsewhere within cost-effective reach in my little craft. So the night before my flight, I get out my aeronautical charts, review the topography and probable route to be followed, calculate time to destination in view of forecast winds aloft, and thereby also determine required fuel.

While not always the first step in exercising leadership, destination determination, i.e. goal setting, should be done from time to time in almost any arena. In commercial, educational, and a variety of other organizational settings these days, the first step in a planning process is typically the development of an overall mission or vision statement. Shortly after my arrival as the new president of the historic Gettysburg Seminary, the board of directors adopted a vision statement that had been under development for some time. It begins: "Bearing witness at the crossroads of history and hope, the Lutheran Theological Seminary at Gettysburg proclaims Jesus Christ to a restless world by preparing our students for faithful discipleship." That vision statement serves us well. In a succinct manner, it states who we are, where we see ourselves now, and our primary objective or destination, namely, the preparation of students for faithful discipleship and Christian leadership in church and world.

In my cross-country planning prior to a flight, I typically find myself mentally flying the course before ever leaving the ground. "I see I'll have to climb fairly high to cross those mountains with a good margin of safety. Ah, yes, that airport has a control tower, so I'll need to call for permission to fly through their airspace. Over here is a high radio transmission tower; I'll need to watch for it and be aware that sometimes during daylight hours the flashing warning lights are turned off. Oh, and in the aftermath of the tragic occurrences of September 11, 2001, with heightened concerns for security, I have to avoid flying over that sports stadium on Saturday afternoons when the local university team is playing a rival." In the very process of cross-country flight planning, some of the most important work in ensuring a successful ultimate outcome is being accomplished.

Likewise, the process whereby an organization develops a mission or vision statement can be almost as important as the ultimate product. Looking around and scanning the environment, examining trends in the surrounding community as well as within the organization, congregation, or other entity are important first steps in charting a course for the future. In the church contexts in which I serve, mission statement development typically involves asking and prayerfully discerning answers to several key questions: Who are we as a community of God's faithful people? What are our strengths and capabilities, as well as our limitations? What are the needs and opportunities to spread God's good news in our immediate context? What are the major and minor trends in the surrounding community, our "mission field" as it were? How are others already meeting needs and providing important services that we should avoid seeking to duplicate? Finally, and most importantly, what is our sense of God's mission in this place, and how can we be partners with others in carrying out God's work?

Various approaches to organizational planning

Once the destination has been determined, i.e. an overall mission or vision statement has been developed, the process of strategic planning for how to get from our present position to the next or final landing point must be carried out. Entire books have been written on various approaches to strategic long-range and more immediate or tactical short-range planning. In a few brief descriptive paragraphs, I will attempt to succinctly summarize four commonly utilized planning methodologies. But first, a definition of planning is in order: *Planning is an organized process of study, reflection, conversation, and writing by which an organization envisions its future, charts a course toward it, and establishes timelines with specific steps to arrive at the preferred destination by efforts congruent with the organization's values.*

1. *SWOT Planning:* This approach to strategic or tactical planning begins with an assessment of an entity's Strengths and Weaknesses, followed by determination of the Opportunities and Threats held out before it in the surrounding environment. SWOT planning gives attention also to how other organizations may be meeting opportunities or minimizing threats.

An advantage of this approach to planning is the affirmation that occurs especially in noting a group's strengths and opportunities; the downside is that focusing too much on weaknesses and threats may paralyze or inhibit creative forward movement.

2. *Needs-based or Constituent-focused Planning:* In this approach to planning, typically some methods of gathering information are determined early on in the process. Often, a survey

instrument or questionnaire is widely distributed to gain feedback from an entity's customers or constituents. "What are your needs, wants, and desires? How can we satisfy them and enhance your experience?" Moving beyond tabulated results from such polling instruments, this approach frequently includes convening a variety of focus groups—gatherings of individuals served by the business or organization—for careful listening on the part of the planners or owners.

The advantages of needs-based planning are readily apparent. People learn they are valued, and their opinions may actually shape an organization's future directions. Planners hear and learn from those who know an organization best "at the grassroots." A primary downside is that such an approach frequently misses the perspectives of those not being served already. An example I have cited in working with many parish governing councils is that a survey of those present at the 10:30 Sunday morning worship service on their preferred time for church may not be very helpful in determining a convenient time for those who can't come at the appointed hour! Likewise, this approach to planning frequently fails to generate truly innovative ideas or genuinely new products. Had the first designers of technological innovations like the microwave oven or walkman radio waited for requests from customers they probably would never have come up with these popular inventions. Few in our society were asking for a better cup of coffee when Starbuck's started marketing its high-end brew. Finally, planners utilizing this approach may need to struggle with their personal and the organization's core values. Simply delivering "what the customer wants" is not always an option if so doing is incompatible with one's fundamental values and ethical principles.

3. *Scenario Development:* Planning in this mode involves a variety of an organization's "stake-holders" (those who hold a stake in its future) in crafting a concrete picture of what the organization might realistically look like at a specified time in the future. Working backward from that desired future state envisioned through strategic visioning, concrete actions steps that will lead toward it are determined in the tactical planning phase. As a consultant with congregations in their planning, I have found this approach particularly engaging. A brief scenario for our school might begin something like: "It is the year 2026, Gettysburg Lutheran Seminary's 200th anniversary. The school has a student body of approximately 500 full- and part-time students ranging in age from 22 to 70 years old. Continuing the pattern of recent years, women outnumber men by a 60/40 ratio. The multicultural campus community is about 1/4 Latino, 1/2 Caucasian, and the rest a mixture of various ethnic groups. The faculty consists of a dozen full-time tenured professors and twice that number of part-time practitioner professors who teach part-time while simultaneously engaging in other vocational settings. The school's budget of $12.5 million is generated through three approximately equal revenue sources of tuition, gifts, and grants, and endowment-generated income."

Strengths of the scenario approach to planning include giving participants the opportunity to produce a concrete mental model of what the organization might look like at a given point in the future. It encourages individuals and groups to move beyond vague generalities ("We want to grow, experience increased income, serve God and our neighbor") typically generated in other types of planning. The pitfalls associated with scenario planning are similar to those cited in #2 above: the truly innovative ideas representing a radical departure from present realities may not surface as planners project the future on the basis of the present status.

4. *Appreciative Inquiry:* This relatively new approach to planning is a labor-intensive method that sends out "scouts" from an organization into a broad array of settings to learn from the experiences of others. As the probing scouts observe and experience life in an organization or context removed from their own, they both affirm those doing good things in that other arena and pick up ideas that may generate their own creativity.

The primary advantage of appreciative inquiry is that it casts the net broadly in search of fresh ideas and "best practices." Dynamic partnerships and strategic alliances may emerge as representatives of an organization are given permission to celebrate the accomplishments of and learn from others' experiences. Possible downsides of the approach are its relatively unfocused nature and the absence of criteria by which to measure the effectiveness of others' projects and their adaptability for implementation by one's own organization.

Some biblical examples of effective planners

As we read the story of Moses leading the Hebrew people out of bondage in Egypt, it seems so simple, doesn't it? Moses, saved by Pharaoh's daughter from Pharaoh's attempt to kill all the Hebrew baby boys, grew up to be a strong young shepherd in the service of his father-in-law, Jethro. One day in the wilderness of Midian, God appeared to him in the form of a burning bush. God said, "I have observed the misery of my people who are in Egypt; I have heard their cry . . . and I have come down to deliver them . . . and bring them up out of that land to a good and broad land" (Exodus 3:7-8). Moses went back to Egypt, joined his Hebrew community, waited for God to send plagues to convince the

Egyptians to free them, and led a grand exodus following the night of the great Passover. Simple, wasn't it? Or maybe not.

The account of Moses and the exodus is clearly presented by the Bible as a story about God's power, not Moses' planning ability. But I do not believe that this account of divine miraculous intervention is diminished by our reflection on human agency and leadership ability. At least in some measure, Moses must have been a very savvy community organizer, a skillful and probably charismatic leader who sat alone or with others many a night by firelight planning. Perhaps he did some form of SWOT analysis. What were the strengths and weaknesses of the Hebrew community? How could they maximize their opportunities to escape and seek to avoid many of the threats the Egyptians kept putting in their way? Or did Moses and his colleagues engage in scenario development? "If the Egyptians do this, then our response is so and so. When we have X number of folks committed to march, then we'll proceed." The sheer logistical planning to lead even a relatively small band of former slaves on an international voyage must have been quite staggering. At least at the outset, they were not planning to rely upon finding wells and manna in the wilderness, so the portage of food and water for both people and animals, provisions for the children, and countless other items were essential. I think if we try to imagine the untold complex history that lies behind the simply told story of the flight of Israel out of Egypt, we can see the hand and heart of a great preflight planner!

While usually not among the many titles ascribed to the one called Lord, Master, Savior, Messiah, Son of Man, and Christ, I think it's worth pondering the nature of Jesus as Planner. At a young and tender age, Jesus apparently began to discern his personal vision and formulate his personal mission: "Did you not know that I must be in my Father's house?" (Luke 2:49b). In his baptism by John at the Jordan, his identity as the beloved child of God was further signaled. Soon he began to carry out his mission of proclaiming the in-breaking reign of God. At some moment, his planning revealed the ultimate destination recorded in the Gospel of Luke: "He set his face to go to Jerusalem" (Luke 9:51). While there would be some course deviations and unintended side trips along the way, the goal remained in sharp focus. Quite simply, he had come to save the cosmos, and that meant meeting his destiny on a cross.

Along the journey to Jerusalem, however, Jesus continued to make multiple midcourse corrections and unscheduled stops. A sick person or a beggar got in his path, deflected the airflow, generated some new lift, and Jesus in turn responded by lifting up those who for so long had been downtrodden. Increasingly, Jesus diverted the long-established customs and cultural flow around him. He began to exert some subtle or not-so-subtle new forces and pressures as he carved out new roles for women, outcasts, and the many regarded as "sinners." Eyes fixed firmly on the ultimate goal, Jesus nevertheless journeyed with flexibility, adapting frequently to changes in the environment or emergency situations encountered along the trip.

For reflection

1. How is planning accomplished in your organization? How might it be improved?
2. As you contemplate your organizational "weight and balance," do you see the need to make any shifts? If so, in what way?
3. Does your congregation or organization have a clear sense of direction? Is your mission statement specific, or is it so generic it could apply to many others?
4. What other great planners from Scripture or Christian history come to mind?
5. As you consider the need to do preflight planning in your congregation or other setting, which of the four strategic planning models would you prefer to use? Why?

3

Cleared for Takeoff

Though it took place three-and-a-half decades ago, I remember as if it were yesterday my very first solo from the grass runway in my hometown of Elbow Lake, Minnesota. My flight instructor, John "Kip" Coleman, who had given me all of nine hours of dual instruction in his Piper Cub, told me to pull over to the side of the runway after we had made three or four takeoffs and landings that brisk March morning in 1968. "Make three on your own," he shouted over the roaring little 90-horsepower engine, "and watch your airspeed."

As I taxied back down that little grass strip, it suddenly dawned on me, "Now, I really have to do this all on my own." With all my 17-year-old bravado, I eased the throttle forward as I had done many times before, nudged the control stick a bit to raise the tail of the little craft. Then, as N7276K built up flying speed, I slowly eased back on the stick. Without Kip's weight in the back seat, that Cub fairly leapt into the air and climbed skyward. I was flying all alone. That day I truly became a pilot!

So it is for anyone who aspires and is granted, or who is nominated and invited by others to assume a leadership position: there comes a time when one must step out and lead. For many, the moment of finally receiving a long-sought call to a leadership post is panic time. "Am I really equipped for this task that I thought I wanted or that has been assigned to me? Can't I just gather at least a little bit more information before making a momentous decision? Please give me the chance to consult a few others who can advise me on the best course to follow. I'm really not equal to the task; to whom can I hand off this responsibility?" But then you look over your shoulder and discover that the back seat is empty! An organization, a business, a congregation, a university, or a work team has designated you the leader, at least on this occasion. It's time either to fly or to take the airplane back to the hangar, shut it down, and hand the mission over to someone else.

Looking back over the course of my nearly three decades of ministerial service, it occurs to me that in each place I have served I did not feel ready for takeoff when I received clearance. My first call was to an inner-city congregation in the heart of central city Los Angeles. Though I had learned some Spanish during my seminary internship in South America, I was not really ready to lead Angelica Lutheran Church in a whole new effort of outreach into a heavily Latino neighborhood. Next followed a call to head a coalition of urban parishes in the San Francisco Bay area, where all the pastors and other key leaders were older and more seasoned than I. How could I possibly emerge as their leader? A few years later a Lutheran bishop invited me to become his assistant and the primary "shepherd" of nearly 60 congregations and 100 ministers, their families and their careers. Job descriptions expanded. For a season while serving on the next bishop's staff, I also was elected president and interim CEO of a large ecumenical council of churches, sitting at the head of tables with bishops, high-powered lay leaders, negotiating with savvy community organizers, federal government contract monitors, and national church executives. About a decade ago a position directing a national church department and being chief staff person for the Conference of Bishops of the Evangelical Lutheran Church in America came my way. I was not ready for it, but I received the appointment and again found myself stretched beyond my gifts and abilities. Most recently, as one who had never served even on the board of an academic institution, to my amazement I was nominated, interviewed for, and then offered the presidency of the oldest and most historic Lutheran seminary in the Americas.

In each of these positions, I felt a sense of God's call being confirmed by those who encouraged me to begin a new ministry. Wonderful people patiently overlooked my inexperience and lack of wisdom, as their new leader probably gave them a bumpy ride in my early months on the job. Many within and from outside the congregation, synod, national church offices, and seminary have stepped up to offer their counsel and mentoring. In each place, I have been enormously blessed by the opportunity to serve for a season of my life.

Considering the "What ifs?"

Before beginning the takeoff roll, a good pilot imagines the departure phase of the flight in his or her mind, pondering all the possible "what ifs?" What if the runway is slippery because of rain or ice? What if the wind conditions are shifting as we gather speed on the takeoff run? What if we're not going fast enough at a predetermined point on the runway? How will I respond if a deer or other animal scampers out of the trees into our path, or if another pilot makes a mistake and gets on the wrong runway? What are the options if an engine falters or a tire blows, or a door suddenly springs open? What if? What if? What if?

In part due to advertisements promoting aviation and seeking to recruit new student pilots, many are convinced that flying an aircraft is roughly equivalent to driving an automobile. Both from my personal experience in learning to fly, and having instructed a handful of others at various stages in their training, I'm convinced that learning to fly is far more taxing than becoming a safe car driver. For one thing, the work involves managing a vehicle in three, not just two dimensions. Given even a small aircraft's greater relative speed, events happen more quickly than in driving a car. The weather, particularly wind, has far greater impact on an airplane than a surface vehicle. Then, too, there's another significant difference between fixed-wing aircraft and automobiles or even helicopters: once airborne, there's no stopping or backing up—you have to keep moving forward!

Leaders in any context do well to constantly contemplate the "what ifs?" Developing several alternatives to solve a problem can help avoid frustration if Plan A doesn't work. Attempting to imagine in advance those things that might divert a group from focusing on its task may assist the leader in fostering progress. In some areas, actually rehearsing how an organization would respond under disastrous conditions can be the key to safety and even survival in a real emergency. "Disaster preparedness" may have broader application than merely holding fire drills on occasion or periodically rehearsing how an emergency room team will respond in the event of a catastrophic tragedy.

Using the checklist

Another critically important discipline for those who pilot airplanes is to use pretakeoff and other checklists. Smart pilots don't simply trust their "smarts"; that's why we use checklists. No matter how many times I have prepared for takeoff in my simple little Cessna aircraft, the next takeoff might be the time I forget to test the magnetos, enrich the mixture, raise the flaps, or call the tower for clearance. In order to avoid overlooking something, I use a checklist. Especially important is checklist use in case of an inflight emergency, and also before landing.

In organizational leadership, the use of written or mental checklists can help a leader avoid overlooking important tasks. Many find helpful a daily or weekly "to do" list, and such are now even routine components of the various electronic calendars and pocket organizers. Task groups stay on track as they develop and monitor timelines with detailed plans for who will do what by when. Having a printed agenda generally helps a committee or work group make the best use of available time and avoid overlooking important discussions or decisions.

While it is rarely written, and frequently developed while driving to a meeting or appointment, I find it helpful to have at least a mental "impact profile" that will keep me focused. I try to ask myself in advance, "What impact do I hope to make with this individual or group over the next hour or by means of this upcoming meeting?" That discipline of a mini-planning process also enables me to evaluate after the fact whether I've achieved my goal or perhaps wasted my time and that of others.

Carefully monitoring the instruments

While a periodic scan of the aircraft instruments by trained watchful eyes is important under all in-flight conditions, it is especially critical in the takeoff phase. As the engines roar to full power, and all the aircraft systems are straining at maximum capacity, component failures are most likely to occur. As speed builds on the runway, demanding primary focus outside the cockpit, it's nevertheless crucial to occasionally glance at the panel and verify that all the engine instruments are "in the green" and that the airplane is developing sufficient airspeed for the takeoff.

In any leadership position, the leader needs to identify the key "instruments" that he or she should monitor to ensure the organization's safety and progress. If recent corporate scandals have taught us anything, they should be alarming reminders of the importance for senior executives and board members to scrutinize financial statements and auditors' reports. Some years ago, a regional unit of our church suffered embezzlement because its leaders trusted too much in the treasurer as he slowly drained the entity of its funds, all the while insisting they didn't need to incur the expense of a formal audit. Sales trends, organization membership statistics, growth or decline in the potential "market" are all important instruments for leaders to monitor.

In many arenas, the most important data is provided through informal networks and associations. Tom Peters' concept of "managing by walking around" (see his book, *In Search of Excellence*) conveys this notion of gathering information and monitoring important signal senders through informal contacts. I advocate and try to practice at least occasionally what I call the "back door discipline." In going to my office on campus, or moving from one meeting to another, I tend to follow the same paths, usually taking the most direct route. On occasion, for no good reason, I go through another door into a building, or take a meandering no-purpose stroll through campus, just to see what I may have been missing by staying on the well-beaten path. I enjoy going incognito to churches or gatherings of church folk to see what I may overhear around the coffee pot, particularly as talk may turn to "the Seminary."

Developing an exit strategy

On rare occasions, when there's a big bang in the engine compartment, or a stray aircraft, vehicle, or creature on the runway, or if the pilot just feels in her or his gut that not everything is right, the prudent course of action is to abort the takeoff while there's still time to stop on the runway remaining. Again, contemplating beforehand the conditions under which the takeoff will be stopped, and knowing the runway marker by which deceleration must be initiated, will prepare the pilot to make a timely go/no-go decision.

Especially when taking on new initiatives or risky ventures, an organization's leaders should develop a pretakeoff "exit strategy."

How and under what conditions should we conclude this isn't working and call a halt? What indicators must we monitor carefully during a planning process to determine whether or not it's the right time to launch our new project? What "runway markers" might we establish as we conduct a feasibility study or marketing survey? What are the critical numbers that tell us launching now won't leave us embarrassed and discouraged?

Again, careful planning is a key in considering exit strategy development. A central principle for savvy community organizers is to identify and help rally interest around winnable causes. Recognizing that a fledgling organization can die in infancy if it experiences even one failure caused by premature action, good organizers take great pains to assure that its initial projects and endeavors will be grand successes. And at the slightest hint that a successful takeoff won't occur, the organizers abort the takeoff through a carefully planned exit strategy.

Acting counter-intuitively can save you

The ultimate adrenaline surge for a pilot on takeoff will occur if and when an engine quits just after liftoff. In a single engine aircraft, your entire source of power has stopped. In a twin- or multiengine airplane, the sudden differential in propulsion and torque requires split-second reaction by the pilot in order to avoid a fiery disaster.

In the case of sudden total loss of power on takeoff, while still close to the ground, the best course is usually to land the airplane straight ahead. The most critical reaction of all is to push the aircraft's nose *down* in order to maintain flying speed and avoid a stall. Doing so, I'm told (for blessedly so far I've been spared the experience) requires every ounce of discipline a pilot can muster. One's instinct is to keep the powerless airplane flying by raising the nose and attempting to stretch the glide. Pushing the nose down while low to the ground is probably akin to forcing one's hand or foot deeper into a scalding pool of water—it goes against every screaming instinct, but in this case it's the key to survival.

While the literature of leadership frequently encourages "trusting one's gut" and going on instinct, I believe there are also times when one must act counter-intuitively in order to do what's best under the circumstances. This is especially the case in times of great stress and under emergency situations. In order to render needed medical attention, emergency services personnel—police, firefighters, paramedics and others—must resist their instinctual recoil and the urge to flee the scene of a gory, gruesome accident. Faced with an angry group of constituents or parishioners, the politician or pastor may best serve them by acting contrary to the very normal human desire to flee the scene. By staying to acknowledge their anxiety, and by listening carefully to their perspectives, the leader may gain added respect and deepen relationships that can become more collaborative in the future.

In his book *Generation to Generation*, Edwin Friedman discusses how, particularly during a state of conflict and high agitation in a "system," it's important for the leader to be "self-differentiated" and to remain a "nonanxious presence." Rather than seeking to persuade others to change their views, suggests Friedman, a leader should chart a course and transparently share, "This is where I'm going and how I'm going to act." While doing so, however, it's critical that the leader also stay connected to individuals and with the entire community.

Scriptural counterintuitive risk-takers

Through the humorous parodies of Bill Cosby and others, the paradoxical behavior of Noah has been recounted. He must have started building the ark during a long season of fair weather! His willingness to listen to God's command to build an ark had to require a huge measure of acting counter to instinct, all the while being subjected to enormous peer pressure and ridicule. Yet, as the story is told in the book of Genesis (chapters 6—9), Noah's faithful response to comply with what he had been called by God to do saved Noah, his family, and the whole human race.

In the New Testament story of Jesus' birth, his parents surely acted contrary to their natural inclinations. Young expectant Mary found the courage to believe the angel Gabriel's preposterous proclamation (see Luke 1:26 ff). Rather than slinking away in shame and despair, she sang a song that has graced all time thereafter with the words of the *Magnificat*. Joseph likewise conducted himself contrary to the expected course of action. Rather than "putting Mary away," quietly calling off the engagement, he embraced her mysterious pregnancy and prepared to father the one who was offspring of the divine. Both Mary and Joseph found the courage to swim against the tide of their cultural conditioning and social expectations. They listened to the voices calling them to forge into untrodden territory.

Time and again, as has been widely noted, Jesus was a counterintuitive risk-taker who acted unconventionally instead of following an easier path to avoid his cross-bound fate. In violation of all cultural conventions and the rules of his society, Jesus interacted with and greatly valued women, children, and others regarded as inferior by the patriarchy that he could have freely embraced and joined. Over and over, when the instincts of self-preservation would have kicked in, Jesus resisted them, acted counterintuitively and moved ahead in his mission.

For reflection

1. Is there a time in your life when you've been "cleared for takeoff" yet hesitated and never moved forward with a project or major commitment? What prevented you?

2. Which instruments in your environment are most critical? Are there some you habitually ignore and need to be monitoring more closely?

3. What items are most important on your checklist? Do you sometimes ignore certain items, exposing yourself and your organization to unnecessary risk?

4. Can you point to a time when you acted counterintuitively, against your instincts or "gut feelings"? Was the outcome good or bad?

5. What critical phase of planning are you presently facing? What do you need to do, or keep in mind (your checklist), as you begin and continue planning?

4

Flying the Airplane

"Fly the airplane," shouted my instructor on numerous occasions during initial training for my private pilot certificate. When roles were reversed and I sat in the right seat as a flight instructor, I repeated the admonition, albeit in a quieter tone through an intercom system, "Fly the airplane." A common variation on this theme of giving priority to remaining in control of the aircraft at all times is, "Either you're flying it, or it's flying you."

Why is there the need for flight instructors to issue this advice to fledgling pilots? Sooner or later, most flyers are overcome with distractions. They get so caught up in talking on the radio, or looking at something on the ground that aircraft control and safety are sacrificed. Such preoccupation with the relatively unimportant is not limited to novice student pilots. On December 29, 1972, a brand new Eastern Airlines wide body L1011 passenger jet crashed into the Florida Everglades killing 101 people. The aircraft was in perfectly fine flying condition. As the giant jet was on final approach to Miami International Airport, an indicator light on the instrument panel that confirms the landing gear is down and locked into position failed to illuminate. Concluding that probably nothing was wrong with the aircraft, the cockpit crew of four became distracted and began trying to replace a $12 faulty bulb. All the while their attention was focused on this nuisance item, the plane was slowly descending until finally it smashed into the swampy Everglades 18 miles northwest of MIA. The cockpit voice recorder recovered after the crash revealed that as it flew closer and closer to the ground, a low altitude warning chime sounded repeatedly. In this instance, a highly trained professional flight crew relinquished their primary task of assuring that at least someone was simply flying the aircraft.

So frequently is distraction and consequent loss of aircraft control the cause of accidents that examiners who issue pilot certificates are mandated during the final qualifying check ride to intentionally introduce distractions. A pencil is dropped on the far side of the cockpit floor, and the license candidate is told to pick it up. Or the examiner will insist that the certificate candidate read minute details on an aeronautical chart. The purpose of these intentional distractions is to determine if the pilot can be coaxed and cajoled to lose focus on basic aircraft control.

"Aviate, navigate, communicate" is a common sequence to remind pilots of relative priorities. Aviate—fly the airplane—is always the highest. Even if at least momentarily the pilot loses awareness of position or direction, the consequences of such a navigational lapse are not likely to be dire. An irked controller on the radio will get over the irritation if the pilot repeatedly ignores radio calls for a few moments. But the loss of aircraft control and resulting stall, spin, or overtaxing its structural load capacity holds the potential for catastrophic consequences.

Leaders maintain priorities

While the consequences may not be as immediate or devastating as a fatal airplane crash, leaders in any sphere who become distracted and lose a clear focus on their essential priority tasks imperil their leadership. In the church's ministry, many well-meaning and generally capable ministers have lost their effectiveness and even their positions by failing to focus on the basic tasks of capably leading services on Sundays, visiting—especially persons who are hospitalized or who have suffered tragedy—and working with others in general administrative oversight of a parish's program. Pastors who get too focused on narrow matters where they have particular interest—highly refined liturgies, minutely micromanaged programs, overuse of computers and other sophisticated technology, or long-term in-depth counseling that benefits only a few—may be in danger of the real or perceived neglect of their basic duties. While this may be tolerated for a while, sooner or later such neglect leads to unrest, and the minister may get in trouble.

Physicians and others who work in emergency rooms or other settings where life-and-death decisions must be made continuously need to develop the ability to prioritize. So also do civic and governmental leaders with budgeting responsibilities. Given limited resources and unlimited needs for human services, infrastructure maintenance, and expanded educational and recreational opportunities, what are the priorities? Once established, adhering to them amidst the continuing clamor for attention by others requires courage and clear focus on the part of leaders.

Scanning: Avoiding fixation

A good flight instructor will also admonish a fledgling pilot to be scanning the sky constantly in all directions. Under visual flight rules, the basic means of avoiding a midair collision with another aircraft is "see and avoid." This means simply that one has to see other aircraft and take any necessary action to avoid a collision. Even in small aircraft flying only 100 miles per hour, the head on convergence with another airplane happens quickly, and prompt avoidance measures are necessary upon spotting a "target" up ahead. Many student pilots have a tendency to "keep their heads inside the cockpit," that is, to over-focus on the flight instruments, aircraft controls, or aeronautical charts. Ignoring the responsibility to spend the vast majority of time scanning the horizon ahead, as well as to the left and right and upward and downward, may eventually result in a pilot's greatest fear—a midair collision.

As an experienced private pilot may progress to pursue an instrument rating, enabling him or her to fly exclusively by means of the aircraft instruments, another kind of scanning is imperative. To safely fly in the clouds, devoid of all external visual references, a pilot must constantly scan all of the flight and engine performance instruments, as well as navigational data from an additional set of gauges. Pilot fixation on one or two instruments to the exclusion of others results quickly in loss of orientation, followed by complete loss of control.

In my experience of observing leaders in many arenas, a similar phenomenon occurs when a leader "loses the scan" and begins to fixate on one or two priorities, tasks, or constituencies, and thereby loses touch with the bigger picture. Preoccupation with the needs of one constituent group may result in ignoring others who aren't demanding as much attention at the moment.

As institutional leaders, it's my colleagues' and my challenge to be constantly maintaining a scan of every dimension of our seminary's life. If we focus too much on student concerns, we may begin to lose touch with the board of directors. Too much concentration on the financial reports, or a constant focus on endowment performance, watching on a daily basis the wild gyrations of the stock market and our investment portfolio, may result in losing contact with faculty and staff needs, the spiritual life of our community, or our public relations and regular communications with alumni, congregations, and supporting individuals.

Situational awareness

Closely related to maintaining a disciplined scan of the entire organization is the importance of staying aware of the surrounding ever-changing situation. Many a pilot and his or her unsuspecting passengers have met their demise, serious injury, or at least grand embarrassment, as a result of the loss of situational awareness. Some years ago, a commercial airliner landed at the wrong destination. Because this relatively small airport's runway was not designed for such a heavy aircraft, the passengers had to be bused to their destination, arriving hours late. In another incident often repeated in aviation lore, two pilots of a jumbo cargo jet flew right over the top of their destination, Los Angeles International Airport, in the wee hours of the morning. Alert air traffic controllers suspecting that the crew had fallen asleep telephoned their company headquarters. Through a series of contacts, the pilots were finally awakened a few hundred miles out over the Pacific Ocean. Fortunately, they had just enough fuel to return for a landing at LAX. While they arrived safely home, I suspect that their loss of situational awareness probably did not advance their flying careers!

Since September 11, 2001, several dozen pilots flying in our local area have faced unforgiving local law enforcement, Federal Aviation Administration, or U.S. Secret Service agents upon landing. In some cases, the landing was "requested" by an F-16 fighter jet that suddenly appeared off a small airplane's wingtip. The reason? Just a few miles south of Gettysburg airport, where my little Cessna is based, lies the P-40 prohibited airspace surrounding the Camp David presidential retreat. For years, this protected portion of the sky had a three-mile radius around the famed mountaintop weekend place of escape from the White House 55 miles to the southeast. In the aftermath of September 11th, with heightened concern for the president's security, the P-40 airspace was expanded to as much as a 10-mile radius. The larger forbidden zone is not depicted on aeronautical charts, so more than a handful of unsuspecting pilots have flown into this no-fly zone, much to their later regret. While none has been shot down by the fighters, the hours-long interrogations and resulting penalties are not pleasant outcomes. In each case, the offending pilot has no doubt pleaded a lack of awareness, either of the airspace's expanded circle, or of his or her exact location relative to Camp David. These multiple instances of the failure to maintain situational awareness have, of course, gained attention in the media and have tended to brand the entire general aviation community, made up of mostly responsible pilots, as reckless threats to national security.

Leaders in business, government, education, health care, social service, or ecclesiastical organizations must likewise seek to maintain the highest possible degree of situational awareness. Where am I? What's going on around me? How are things changing, and how does such change impact us? These and others are the constant questions required to maintain an appropriate level of situational awareness.

Accepting decision-making responsibility

A particularly insidious temptation encountered by pilots of all experience levels is to rely overly much on the counsel and commands of air traffic controllers. More than a few pilots can relate stories of being told to "turn left and descend to 3,000 feet" only to discover that complying with the controller's instruction would result in flying head-on into a mountainside! It is not that the controllers are intentionally attempting to cause a tragic disaster. But they are human and on rare occasions make very human mistakes. A good pilot, therefore, is constantly second-guessing a controller's instructions, verifying that compliance with a command will result in a safe and responsible course of action. Good flight instructors imbue in their students the willingness and fortitude to respond "unable" if a controller's command is unreasonable or unsafe.

In any context, leaders can become overly dependent upon others when it comes to decision-making. In many cases, such paralyzing indecision may plague leaders who are relatively new in their positions. "I don't know enough yet to make this decision." "Surely, the board of directors or long-time staff persons know what's going on and I can trust their advice." Such are common reactions on the part of a new leader faced with a crisis. While making precipitous and unilateral decisions can impede progress and damage collaboration, so too can repeated responses of "I don't know enough yet to make that decision." Especially in a large organization, deferring major decisions or attempting to delegate them to others who lack authority in the system can be paralyzing and demoralizing behavior on the part of senior leaders.

An organization that I had opportunity to observe closely seemed for years to have a severe case of "consultantitis." That is to say, they went from one management consultant to another, always in search of the perfect way to "re-engineer" and restructure. Those of us who regularly worked with the organization found ourselves frustrated, never knowing who would be our contact persons from month to month. It seemed as if decisions were always being deferred as leaders waited for the perfect solution to be revealed to them by some outside guru. In any context, there finally comes a time when leaders have to lead, when decisions must be made. Hoping that "someone else" will make the tough calls, or awaiting further revelation that is just around the next corner often produces worse results than premature decision-making by inexperienced leaders who lack all the facts.

Always looking ahead: Being accountable to the future

Among those who fly there is a pithy little query, "What are the two most important things for a pilot?" The unexpected answer for first-time recipients of the question is, "the next two things." Here the idea is reinforced that a pilot must not only establish priorities, keep up the scan, maintain situational awareness and assume ultimate responsibility for what's happening in the moment, but s/he also does well to be constantly anticipating what's coming next. Beyond the next two things, the pilot should also be thinking farther down the flight path to anticipate how s/he will cope with weather, manage fuel, begin a descent and approach the destination, and perhaps fly a challenging instrument approach through marginal atmospheric conditions. Waiting until one is already amidst those conditions can leave the pilot overwhelmed and unable to cope with the demanding workload. Under challenging circumstances, the results of a failure to plan ahead can be disastrous. Thus, "staying ahead of the airplane" is crucial.

Leadership in the fast-paced, rapidly changing context of the 21st century calls for the same discipline of constantly looking farther ahead than comes naturally. I believe that leaders are not just partially responsible for what's happening in the present, but are deeply and profoundly accountable to the future. Let me repeat: leaders are accountable to the future. In our frantic consumer society where we leverage assets, incur ever-increasing indebtedness, gobble nonrenewable resources, and defer much-needed maintenance on our infrastructure, we seem to live as if there is no tomorrow. From our televisions, magazines, and Internet advertisements, we are constantly bombarded with messages to "go for broke," "have it your way now," expect "no boundaries", and the like. Our political leaders run up the national debt, fail to guarantee the future of our Social Security system, avoid legislating even stricter environmental preservation measures, and in other ways enable us to splurge today, mindless of the cost to ourselves later and to our children and grandchildren decades down the road.

In early 2003, nearly every chief executive of an educational institution is wrestling to cope with budget deficits resulting from severe downturns in the economy and stock market, which in turn have caused our endowment values to plummet, and annual receipts to decline in many schools. In response, many college and university presidents, as well as those who head smaller schools like my own, are faced with tough decisions. Do we reduce expenditures, raise tuition, and launch new fund-raising efforts? Do we contemplate personnel reductions when we're already understaffed, and cause hardship and personal pain to those whose jobs are eliminated? Or do we proceed with business as usual, counting on a turnaround in the economy that will bail us out before reserves are depleted and endowments are eroded to the point that the future of our institutions may be jeopardized?

Believing that we are accountable to the future, the leaders of the institution where I serve are seeking to contain costs and maintain a balanced budget without dipping deeper into our endowment principle. We believe that while we are obligated to serve the present generation, we must also be good stewards for the sake of future generations of students, and for churches that will need leaders 50 and 100 years from now. Tempting as it is to spend more now and leave worries about the long-term fiscal viability of the institution to our successors, we see it as our responsibility to pass along as many resources as possible. Even as we try to meet the needs of the present generation of students, faculty, staff, and our many constituents, we attempt also to hold ourselves accountable to the future.

Some biblical examples of prudent decision-makers

While the commonly held mythology that surrounds pilots often pictures them as heroic adventurers who keep an aircraft aloft by their sheer brilliance and physical prowess, the reality is that, above all, pilots are prudent decision-makers who exercise good judgment. Pondering faithful leadership in the 21st century, I find myself circling around a couple of biblical narratives wherein the players demonstrated wise and responsible decision-making, and exercised the disciplines of scanning and looking far up ahead on the journey.

At the young age of thirty, Joseph had found favor with Pharaoh and was given authority over the entire land of Egypt (see Exodus 41). Through careful discernment, reading the signs of the times, looking way down the road, and holding himself accountable to the future, Joseph determined that a season of plenty would be followed by a prolonged drought. Rather than proceeding with business as usual, Joseph initiated a comprehensive nationwide program of gathering grain and carefully stewarding its storage. As a result, not only were the people of Egypt enabled to survive the years of drought when neighboring peoples perished, he saved his family and achieved a grand reunion and reconciliation with his estranged brothers who once had sold him into slavery.

Even Joseph, however, had his limits as a leader. Eventually, he became greedy, accumulating more and more wealth for himself and Pharaoh, while consigning his fellow Israelites to a state of slavery that would persist until the Exodus when another visionary leader named Moses would help a people set out in search of freedom. So a final lesson about leadership may be learned from the Joseph story. Leaders need to be constantly on guard against their own unhealthy appetites and tendencies to be self-serving rather than focusing on the needs and best interests of those they lead. In the end, Joseph lost his scan of the big picture and failed to see the disastrous results of enslaving the Hebrew people.

In the New Testament, there is a rather obscure character who seldom figures prominently in Bible studies or Sunday school lessons. Yet I have long admired this visionary big-picture Pharisee who looked far down the road into the future and encouraged his colleagues' prudent course of action in the moment.

In the fifth chapter of the book of Acts, it is reported that the apostles of Jesus had been going full throttle in their ministries of healing, preaching, and doing many other signs and wonders. Their popularity had become threatening to the high priests and other religious authorities, who called together a council that decided to put the apostles in the public prison. Following a miraculous escape that enabled them to resume their public ministry, the apostles were again hauled before the council where they declared, "We must obey God rather than any human authority" (Acts 5:29). Enraged, the council members were on the verge of becoming a lynch mob. Amidst this chaotic, highly charged atmosphere, one calm voice, that of Gamaliel, a respected teacher and wise counselor, urged a different course. "Fellow Israelites," he began, "consider carefully what you propose to do to these men" (Acts 5:35). Gamaliel went on to reflect upon a couple of historic situations in which popular rabble rousers had come to naught when left to their own devices. Turning to the situation at hand, Gamaliel counseled restraint, saying, "If this plan or this undertaking is of human origin, it will fail; but if it is of God, you will not be able to overthrow them—in that case you may even be found fighting against God" (Acts 5:38-39).

Amidst the confusion and frenzy generated by those who could focus only on their own emotions in the passion of the moment, Gamaliel's leadership generated lift that enabled the entire council to view the future from a higher plane. His ability to scan the skies up ahead, to see the larger systemic picture, to hold himself and the group accountable to the future, and to trust that an unseen divine player was at work changed the course of history for the Christian community and for the whole world.

For reflection

1. What are some major distractions in a typical work week for you? How can you avoid becoming fixated on the wrong things?
2. What are the essentials in your life that must receive priority over all else?
3. Are there persons to whom you relinquish too much of your personal power and authority? How is it that they lull you into an inappropriate dependency?
4. As a steward accountable to the future, to what must you say "no" today in order to serve the longer term interests of your community?
5. Think of a task you wish to accomplish, or a goal you wish to reach. Envision the successful completion or fulfillment of the task or goal. What could keep you from accomplishing your goals? How will you deal with the potential roadblocks?

5

Crew Resource Management: Team Piloting

Over the past two decades, a whole new dimension has emerged in pilot training and the preparation of leaders for airline cockpit environments. Hundreds of aviation-related psychologists and other observers of human interactions have studied how pilots go about the work of flying airplanes. Riding along in cockpits or observing pilots flying sophisticated simulators that replicate airliners in all imaginable flight conditions, these students of aviators have learned a great deal about teamwork or the lack thereof among crews of two or more pilots. Accident investigators of the National Transportation Safety Board, together with officials of the Federal Aviation Administration, airline executives, and aircraft manufacturers have teamed up to share their insights from poring over accident reports, listening to tapes recording final conversations before a crash, and reviewing other information provided by the infamous "black boxes" recovered from most major crash sites. All of this research has contributed to the substantial and growing body of knowledge commonly referred to in pilot training manuals and workshops as "crew resource management" (formerly called "cockpit resource management").

In brief, crew resource management (CRM) advocates a stance of encouraging pilots to take advantage of and utilize all available resources, especially the human resources at their disposal. Flyers of small single-pilot aircraft are encouraged to view their passengers as resource persons, enlisting them to watch for other aircraft, look for prominent checkpoints on the ground, change radio frequencies, or assist the pilot with other simple cockpit tasks and duties. Even children can be enlisted and are usually eager to help, thereby gaining a sense of contributing to the effort of flying an airplane. When the small plane pilot flies solo, s/he frequently still has resource persons available via radio. In a large aircraft, each member of a multipilot crew is expected to be a team player contributing to the overall success of every flight. Airline training programs spend considerable time and energy on CRM, helping every member of a cockpit crew maximize his or her ability to contribute to a successful outcome of each and every flight.

Good teams don't just happen

Those who train pilots realize that good teamwork doesn't just occur without conscious effort. How can a team go about its own development, foster continuing growth, and sustain itself over time? In the first place, at least one person on the team has to have either explicit or tacit responsibility for team maintenance and development. Many times, the one designated as leader (chief executive, highest officer, dean, teacher, professor, senior pastor, or elected or appointed chairperson) fulfills this role. But for other teams, one who is not the designated leader or convener might be the official or unofficial tender of relationships and the one who gives special attention to the life of the group itself. What is the role of such a person? It will, of course, vary by context. But it's important that at least one person periodically call a team to reflect upon its own group life.

Working teams do well to plan periodic retreats or other extended sessions that include not just more time for regular business or planning, but also components that are intentionally aimed at building the team. Such times can be fun as well as intense. To be effective, they should gently encourage a measure of appropriate self-disclosure; by getting to know one another better, effective team members enhance their synergy and expand their collective overall ability to achieve their purposes and fulfill their missions. What are some practical ways by which working teams can deepen their collegiality and foster more effective working partnerships? To be sure, there are books and other resources offering a host of team-building exercises. One of the most effective I have found, and one that seems to resonate especially with faith-based groups, is a gifts identification exercise. We begin with a blank sheet of newsprint, randomly select one member of the group, and then pose the question, "What are Mary's gifts?" Usually, if group members know each other fairly well, it doesn't take long to fill an entire sheet with a list of adjectives, verbs and nouns, or short phrases. This exercise affirms the named individual and enables the rest of the team members to take mental note of Mary's attributes and gifts, and draw on them as they carry out their work. Many other more sophisticated instruments are available to help members of a work team understand what makes each other tick. With the guidance of a trained consultant, many teams have found a tool such as the Myers-Briggs Personality Inventory to be useful in team building.

As a seminary, in addition to our primary focus on students seeking degrees, we seek increasingly to meet the needs and desires of many persons who have committed themselves to the notion of "lifelong learning." As a corporate body, we seek to be a learning organization. Our administrative planning council begins each meeting with a "learning time." One member of the council is invited to lead us in a discussion for 45 minutes or so, typically on a topic somehow related to our work. On occasion, however, we roam far afield, focusing on the big picture of global events or societal megatrends. Sometimes we distribute a brief article or

other background materials in advance, expecting a bit of prepara-
tory "homework" to help us move quickly into discussion. By means
of these monthly in-house seminars, we seek to expand our knowledge and strengthen our team. Likewise, we are attempting to offer
more opportunities in our faculty meetings for professors to teach
one another, sharing from their respective areas of expertise.

Common traits of effective team players

Those whose responsibility it is to hire pilots for airline flight
crews bear an enormous burden. Indirectly, their hiring decisions
affect the lives of thousands of people. Even one "bad hire" can
result in a disaster. Airline human resources personnel charged
with hiring pilots know that any candidate selected for an inter-
view has the requisite ratings, piloting experience, and ability to
fly an airplane with skill and precision. What they are most looking for in an applicant, accordingly, is the all-important but diffi-
cult-to-measure qualities of good decision-making and judgment.
Since any airline flight situation involves at least a two-pilot cockpit crew working with flight attendants, ground personnel, air
traffic controllers, and many others, those who hire pilots are also
attempting to discern an applicant's ability and inclination to
work in a team. Lone ranger pilots may do fine as crop dusters or
bush pilots, but they are seldom an asset in an airline cockpit.

Are there some attributes and attitudes common among successful team players? Five are suggested here as a beginning list,
with readers encouraged to offer additional traits from your experience and observation of successful team players.

First, the willingness to be *committed to a common vision* is
probably the foremost requisite quality. If we can't agree on the
destination, then how can we ever pilot our organization to where
it needs to go? This ability to make a commitment to a collective

vision often entails the willingness to compromise. No two human beings, even a long-married couple, ever see things entirely in the same way. No two pilots will fly the same airplane in quite the exact same way. Insisting on one's own way, particularly in a fast-paced and high-stakes environment like an airline cockpit, can have devastating results. A captain who seeks to micromanage her or his first officer's every move will cause the copilot to be distracted and uncomfortable at the controls. Tell me that the pilots up front are a rigid, uncompromising duo, both of whom just came from horrendous spats at home, and I'll unbuckle my seat belt, run toward the doorway shouting, "Let me out!"

In any arena of leadership, a second personal trait necessary for teamwork is a simple *willingness to spend time together*. In the course of my working life, I have known some individuals who are natural introverts, who abhor meetings, fail to respond to routine daily communications from coworkers, and otherwise isolate themselves from the group. As already noted, for a group of individuals to form a working team, each participant must recognize that a necessary part of the work is that of relationship building and maintenance over time. In working with conflicted situations over the years, I have discovered over and over again that at the root of the conflict is the simple reality that the coworkers-turned-combatants simply don't take the time to listen to each other, understand respective points of view, and forge mutually agreeable courses of action.

A third key identifier of those who can be effective team players is a *lack of defensive turf-protection*. While it's important that each person have a carefully delineated job description, be it written or less formally defined, beware the person who says too often, "That's not my job!" In good teams there is a certain fluidity, a degree of permeability and a spirit of cooperation. Rather than reacting from the default position of, "That's not in my job description," the good team player is constantly asking of coworkers, "How can I support you in your work?" Just as an amateur baseball or softball team is well served by having a large number of utility players who are moderately good at several positions, most working teams benefit by having several persons who can move back and forth into several functions. Cross-training, i.e. encouraging team members to learn as much as they can about each others' jobs, enhances a team's ability to cope when there's a crisis, when a key player is suddenly absent due to illness or for other reasons. I encourage members of my staff to ask themselves the sobering question, "If I'm hit by a truck or felled by a heart attack, who will have the information and know-how to carry on so that the entire organization isn't paralyzed by my sudden absence?"

The fourth attribute of good collaborative workers is the flip side of the previous one. Team players *respect one another's boundaries*. While a measure of fluidity aids teamwork, lack of boundaries creates chaos and frustration. Most of us probably have experienced a coworker in some environment who seems to want to do everyone else's job, or at least closely scrutinize and supervise every other colleague's efforts. In this sense, the ability to judiciously determine and express that "John makes those calls, and I respect his judgment," or "It's Mary's job to make those decisions and carry out her tasks as she sees fit" is essential to healthy teamwork. Especially important is the commitment and determination to respect personal boundaries, particularly regarding sexuality in the workplace. Suffice it simply to mention here that failure to avoid all forms of sexual harassment and abuse is absolutely devastating in any arena.

A fifth and final characteristic of good team players, and one that is increasingly important in our multicultural world of the 21st century, is that they *seek and value diversity*. Gone are the days when homogeneous groups of folks who look, speak, act, and think the same are optimal or even desirable. We live in a world of great and growing diversity. Thought by some to be a problem to be avoided, diversity ought to be sought and celebrated as a gift. Groups that are all of one gender or made up of persons of one racial or ethnic group may be fine under certain circumstances. But the more a group can embrace persons from different backgrounds, give voice to all members, especially those historically absent or silent (women, persons of color, youth, etc.), the better equipped a leadership team will be to embrace today's world and to lead effectively in any arena.

Flying the right seat—a special grace

In any aircraft, large or small, the left front seat belongs to the pilot in command. The final responsibility for the safe conduct of the flight is in her/his hands. In a context where decisions sometimes must be made in a split second, and where two pilots tussling over who makes the final call can have dire consequences, this leadership hierarchy defining "where the buck stops" is probably necessary. In many other teamwork environments, it is less important to have at all times one person designated as being the boss, the one in charge. Nevertheless, in most organizations, especially large and complex institutions where there may be a plethora of opinions and judgments about the right course of action, holding one individual as finally accountable for overseeing the overall life and work of the community is usually advisable.

While having a left seat pilot in command is necessary for an airline crew to function optimally, are all those right seat occupants lesser beings who should grovel in subservience to the pilot in command? Not at all! In fact, the work of a competent first officer or copilot is no less critical for the safe conduct of a modern airliner's flight than that of the captain. Contrary to common misperception, the copilot does a lot more than just "assisting the pilot." In most aircrews, the two front-seat pilots trade off flying duties on each leg of a trip. Thus, the captain may do the takeoff, landing, and all other actual flying duties on the first leg, with the first officer assuming those duties on the next. The nonflying pilot generally handles radio communication, navigation duties, and conducts a continual overall monitoring of the flying pilot's work, while also joining in watching the skies for other aircraft and scanning the instruments as well. This built-in redundancy and respectful second-guessing makes it less likely that a flying pilot's mistakes go undetected, or that some critical items on a checklist are missed.

Another common public misconception is that the left seat pilot is necessarily the more experienced and overall most competent person in the cockpit. Since both pilots must be fully trained and capable to fly the aircraft single-handedly in case of incapacitation of the other, and since it can be virtually impossible to assign final responsibility on the basis of relative competence, pilots assume captain status on the basis of a seniority system. When your name rises to a certain number on the pilot roster, you can bid to qualify for captain. Until you reach that place on the list, no matter how good a pilot you are, you'll remain in the right seat. Placement on the pilot roster is strictly on the basis of when one is hired, with no preference assigned because of prior experience or total flying hours, etc. Accordingly, it's not uncommon for the captain to have less flying experience than the one sitting in the right seat as copilot. In some cases, the first officer may be an overall more competent pilot than the captain.

From personal experience, and through observing others in secondary leadership positions, I am convinced that it takes a special grace to be the one who flies the right seat. Much of my ministry in the church has been as an associate pastor and assistant to four bishops. For nearly twenty years, I was an "assistant to" the one who bore ultimate responsibility and had to make the final calls on the big decisions. While each of my bosses was graceful and supportive, rarely overriding my decisions, nevertheless I recognized that my role was as adviser and assistant. In a couple of these positions, one of the roles I fulfilled was that of "ghost writer." A busy chief executive simply doesn't have time to respond to every item of correspondence or write every speech, report, and article that s/he must present. A chief executive must be surrounded by a capable cadre of assistants who are graceful and humble enough to do the bulk of the work on a piece of legislation, a speech, or report, recognizing that all credit (and of course any blame, too) will be given to the boss.

Another critical role for a right-seat person is to be an unapologetic truth teller who gives honest feedback to the chief executive, president, or other senior leader. In countless airline and other accident investigations involving multipilot crews, it was determined that the first officer or perhaps a flight engineer in the cockpit realized that things were going awry. But either because of copilot timidity, or a kind of unapproachable, authoritarian attitude projected by the captain, the one who could have saved the day failed to speak up. As a result, a key dimension of CRM training these days includes scenarios and exercises designed to promote appropriate assertiveness on the part of right-seat pilots, and to instill in the left-seat captain an attitude of collaborative openness and eagerness to get feedback from her/his flying partners.

Particularly dangerous are right-seat pilots aspiring to "move over" by means of undermining the captain's leadership. Thinking that if the captain "crashes" and is out of the picture, there will be a spot for me in the captain's seat" is flawed for obvious reasons! As one progresses in a field of endeavor or career it is only natural that one may aspire to be the lead person. Such aspirations are worthy, and organizations do well in encouraging individuals to grow into positions of greater responsibility and influence. But an assistant, vice president, or other associate who hopes to assume the lead position by undermining, second-guessing, or criticizing the current incumbent is both detrimental to the organization and likely to damage rather than enhance his/her opportunities for advancement. One who is constantly dissatisfied with the style or decisions of the lead person probably is best advised to move on from that organization.

Of course, there may be rare occasions when direct intervention by the right-seat person is necessary. It's a fascinating discussion, I'm told, when a group of airline first officers or copilots turn to considering conditions under which they might seize control, or even take necessary steps to temporarily incapacitate a captain who is under the influence of drugs or alcohol, has had a mental breakdown, or given way to suicidal or even homicidal urges. Fortunately, such occurrences are almost unheard of due to the careful initial screening and constant monitoring of those entrusted with the lives of hundreds of people. If a supervisor is abusing the power of office, embezzling funds, or engaging in other unethical behavior, incapacitated by untreated addiction, or sexually harassing others in the workplace, his/her subordinates not only may but should take whatever steps are necessary to call the leader to account. In rare cases, where direct confrontation with the offending individual may prove unsuccessful or be unsafe for the subordinate, "going over the boss's head" to a superior in the organization or even a board of directors may be the responsible course of action.

Debriefing and getting feedback

One of the most important phases of flight training is often routinely skimmed over or skipped altogether by busy, harried flight instructors—the postflight debriefing session with a student pilot.

Spending even a few minutes together after a training flight analyzing what went well and what areas needed improvement, and which maneuvers the student understood and where s/he has doubts or questions, is essential in making the most of a lesson. For experienced pilots too, whether they fly the space shuttle or a tiny single engine aircraft, engaging in self-reflection and debriefing with peers is a key in continuing to hone skills and maintain positive, safe attitudes. So critical is such periodic feedback and objective assessment of a pilot's flying abilities and attitudes that it is mandated both by law and company policies for those who fly commercially. Those of us who fly primarily for pleasure or for our own travel must hire a flight instructor every two years to conduct a comprehensive flight review of our skills and competency to continue exercising the privileges of our licenses. Wise pilots, especially those who fly infrequently, recognize the importance and value of periodic refresher courses and of flying with more experienced pilots in order to gain feedback and expanded knowledge.

In any teamwork environment, it is important to engage in periodic debriefing sessions in which team members assess an event, major project, or crisis situation. What can we learn from this experience? Where did we do well and how might we do an even better job the next time? How was our teamwork?

An annual performance review or evaluation has become standard in many workplaces. Unfortunately, what applies for all other staff or employees is sometimes overlooked for the chief executive or others in senior leadership positions. It's critical for the top leaders to set the tone, insisting upon regular evaluation by the board of directors or others to whom they report. In many cases, peer review is required, asking colleagues from outside organizations who inhabit similar leadership posts to lend their aid in giving feedback and making suggestions for improvement.

Biblical examples of teamwork

Recalling lessons from the Bible I learned in Sunday school classes, I remember that instruction being focused on the great heroic figures of the faith. In fact, my earliest remembrances are of a series of little folders, each telling the story of one great biblical hero from The Old or New Testament. We heard the story of this giant in Judeo-Christian history, and then we were given the opportunity to color a picture of the heroic leader chosen by God for some great action.

I wonder if this approach to teaching Scripture may have imbued in generations of church members and leaders an unarticulated, even unconscious set of assumptions about leadership. Many in the church today who are entrusted with overseeing its work—bishops, denominational executives, seminary professors, and others—express a concern that far too many of our clergy still seem to function as "lone rangers" in their ministries. Not only do some ministers seldom collaborate or gain support from their clergy colleagues, but a certain percentage seem to have great difficulty working collaboratively with the members of their congregations. Study after study identifies a pastor's isolationist or unilateralist tendencies as a major contributor to conflict in congregations of all denominations.

One of the Bible stories I loved as a child and still return to often, however, tells of two women of different generations and from diverse backgrounds who bound themselves together as traveling companions and co-creators of a new kind of partnership. When exhorted by her mother-in-law Naomi to remain in her native homeland, Ruth protested, "Do not press me to leave you or to turn back from following you! For where you go, I will go; where you lodge I will lodge; your people shall be my people, and your God my God" (Ruth 1:16). Ruth's marvelous declaration of affection for Naomi has inspired countless generations of the faithful to strive for collaboration, whether in marriage or other family configurations, or in communities that embrace diversity and strive for true partnership on the part of all members.

In the New Testament, the disciples of Jesus seem finally to have become a team when they set about their missionary task in the earliest days of the church's life following the Lord's crucifixion and resurrection. While they often had been competitive and even contentious with each other during their days on the road with Jesus, once he gave them the great missionary command to "go and make disciples," they appear to have recognized the imperative nature of supporting one another and working as a team. In the fourth chapter of Acts, it is reported:

> Now the whole group of those who believed were of one heart and soul, and no one claimed private ownership of any possessions, but everything they owned was held in common. With great power the apostles gave their testimony to the resurrection of the Lord Jesus, and great grace was upon them all. (Acts 4:32-33)

What was undoubtedly some form of socialistic sharing went far beyond the common ownership of material goods. Being of "one heart and soul" was a radical expression of teamwork. Surely, it was not without its challenges. But at some point, in the aftermath of Jesus' resurrection, when they could no longer depend upon the master to mediate their squabbles, it seems as though the disciples holed up for a good long retreat, assessed candidly one another's gifts, assigned respective tasks to be accomplished, determined to collaborate, and then set out on their mission of sharing the good news with the whole world.

For a final example of a team player mentioned in Scripture, I reminisce about an exhortation given to me in the spring of 1981, when I was installed as the pastor/director of a coalition of urban Lutheran churches in the San Francisco Bay area. The preacher for the installation service was our bishop, the Rev. Stanley E. Olson. In his sermon, the bishop suggested that my calling as one who would serve among dozens of clergy and lay leaders in mostly small, scrappy, resource-challenged congregations was to be like *Syzygus,* an obscure biblical character mentioned only once in the fourth chapter of Philippians. The Greek name is translated into English as either "loyal companion" or "true yokefellow" (see Philippians 4:3). In that coalition ministry, and each place where I have served since, I have often recalled the good bishop's counsel and challenge, seeking to be a good team player. Often I have failed, to be sure, but the goal remains to join with others in advancing the mission entrusted to us.

For reflection

1. As you contemplate the various teams in which you collaborate—at work, in your church or volunteer activity—which are most fun and which ones drag you down? Why?

2. What are the most challenging aspects of your teamwork these days? Have you and your coworkers discussed recently how to improve your collaboration?

3. Think of a time when you have "flown the right seat" in some venue. How did it feel? Would you prefer to be the one in charge? If you aren't, how do you deal gracefully with your subordinate status?

4. If you are the lead person in your team, how do you encourage your colleagues and support their work and personal development? Can they challenge you and tell the truth as they see it?

6

Landings Are
the Hardest Part!

Over the years, as a new acquaintance learns of my avocation as a pilot, almost invariably the question will arise, "What's the hardest part?" Without hesitation, I answer, "Landings." Most nonflyers intuitively surmise this to be the case, although many are surprised when a pilot compares the relative difficulty of takeoffs and landings. The former pretty much happen by themselves, with a little coaxing by the pilot; the latter requires a combination of planning, precision, and no small amount of just plain good luck, especially for a perfect landing when one "greases it on!"

In a cockpit of any size, an observer can sense the heightened energy as the pilot begins preparing for landing. Most sit up straighter in their seats. Any nonessential chatter between pilots ceases. We begin organizing things, setting radio frequencies, consulting charts and instrument approach procedures, and reviewing the all important pre-landing checklist. An even sharper scan must be maintained for other aircraft as we know all planes in the area are probably converging toward the same runway. At a tower-controlled field, the pace of conversation between pilots and the control tower accelerates as the controllers help pilots plan their approaches to mesh with other traffic. The landing approach requires the combination and simultaneous application of a complex set of skills to slow the aircraft's speed, maintain a controlled descent to the runway, execute a series of turns while descending, manage frequent radio communications with the approach controller and tower, lower flaps, make power setting changes, adjust for varying wind conditions, and be constantly on the lookout for other aircraft. Among pilots, there's a cryptic summary about landings: any one you walk away from is a good one, and if they can use the plane again it's a great one! This old adage recognizes the difficulty of making a perfect landing. It's a word of encouragement to us all when we bounce a bit, hit the runway just a tad harder than planned, or occasionally have to execute a "go around" and try the whole thing over again. A pilot who strives for a perfect landing every time can soon become disillusioned and dispirited. The "walk away standard" allows for some self-forgiveness, though one must never become complacent or allow safety to be compromised by becoming lackadaisical about landings.

Ending well and preparing for one's successor

Many an otherwise good leader diminishes her or his legacy by beginning to slough off in the final phases of a task or sojourn in a particular place. We've all witnessed such persons who provide solid, strong, and even extraordinary leadership for years. But the last few months on the job, things begin to fray at the edges. Some meetings are skipped; phone calls are not returned. Perhaps one who scrupulously managed expenditures to stay within budget loses interest and allows some "extras" here and there. Planning for the future may cease altogether for a leader who falls victim to short-timers syndrome.

It is only natural that one who is preparing to move on to a new leadership post or into retirement will begin to focus on the future at some point. A certain amount of letting go may be healthy for the organization. The opposite—moving into a hyper-controlling stance, seeking to lock into place a whole program for the next several years—may prove limiting to the next leader who will want a degree of freedom to shape new directions and to lead in his or her own way.

Along with maintaining a proper balance between prematurely abdicating one's leadership on the one hand, and overfunctioning in one's last days in a particular setting on the other, it's crucially important that a departing leader express gratitude and say good-bye to all those who have been partners in that place. A marvelous little book by Roy Oswald, *Running Through the Thistles* (Alban Institute Publication, 1978) conveys to ministers and other religious leaders the importance of saying a proper good-bye. Those who seek to minimize the pain of departing by skipping town without a round of intentional good-byes, says Oswald, may leave unfinished business and untended feelings that can haunt the work of one's successor, as well as make it difficult for the leave-taker to plunge into new endeavors.

So a happy landing at the end of a successful stint of leadership requires finding an appropriate balance—neither becoming irresponsible by relinquishing too much authority and influence prematurely, nor tying the hands of one's successor by a last minute flurry of activities intended to set long-range directions. Finally, a good ending includes saying a proper good-bye to all those who have been good and faithful partners along the journey.

While some pilots are fortunate enough to own their own airplanes, the vast majority rent aircraft flown by many others. In this arena, proper etiquette upon completing a flight includes leaving the airplane tidy and full of fuel for the next pilot. Even more important than properly cleaning and securing the aircraft is to note in its records any "squawks" or items needing maintenance attention, especially if they might compromise safety on subsequent flights. Pilots who rush home from the airport leaving an aircraft dirty, unfueled, unlocked, and without all equipment in its proper position soon develop a reputation around the airport, and may even be denied future rentals if their shoddiness compromises safety.

An effective leader who is a good steward begins preparing for the leadership of her or his successor the first day on the job. Strange as that may sound, I am convinced it is true. What does this mean in practical terms? In the first place, I believe it means that a good leader seeks to solve problems as they arise, take care of business in a timely fashion, and avoid postponing and deferring major decisions into the far distant future. We can probably all think of examples where a major problem went unsolved during the entire multiyear tenure of a leader.

Secondly, preparation for one's successor means avoiding exercising leadership in such a way as to send a message to one's supervisees and colleagues that there's only one way to do things. Criticizing one's predecessor, ridiculing colleagues in similar leadership posts and other defensive attitudes begin to convey the message that my way is the only way. Small wonder, then, that after my departure things may be rough for my successor who surely will do some things differently.

In my work with congregations in pastoral leadership transition, I have seen both good and bad examples of clergy preparing the way for their successors. In a few cases, a premature disengagement left a parish groping to find its way for months while the outgoing pastor still remained in office and on the payroll. Anger began to build and often went unresolved, only to descend in a fury upon the new minister shortly after s/he arrived on the scene. At the other extreme, I have witnessed retiring clergypersons exercise an inappropriate degree of control over everything, including the process of choosing their successor. Congregational members were either subtly or overtly given a message that there's only one right way to do things. The conditions are ripe under such circumstances for the next minister to encounter conflict early on as at least some minor things will inevitably be done in a new way.

Upon assuming my present post I was welcomed graciously by my immediate predecessor. At my request, we had a brief overlap period during which he introduced me to key constituent groups and briefed me on critical current situations requiring my immediate attention. Another predecessor lives in the local community and likewise offers his constant gracious support and encouragement. What a gift when those who have gone before us are chief among our encouragers and cheerleaders!

Biblical landings

Among my favorite passages in all Scripture, the 11th chapter of Hebrews offers a long list of leaders who remained faithful until their calls were completed and they moved on into the larger life of God. Unfortunately, the names are almost all masculine, so we must gaze more deeply into the stories and imagine also the women leaders among God's people. All of those biblical figures we have considered in previous chapters appear to have ended their ministries faithfully. That the church lives on in our own time is testimony to their ending well and preparing the way for successors, passing the mantle of leadership from one generation to the next.

The Bible ends on a note of hope. One more time in the book of Revelation, there is a bending of the flow of history, lifting our sights in a God-ward direction:

"See, I am making all things new! . . . The one who testifies to these things says, 'Surely I am coming soon.' Amen. Come, Lord Jesus! The grace of the Lord Jesus be with all the saints. Amen." (Revelation 21:5 and 22:20-21)

For reflection

1. As you ponder your own "landings," have they been good ones? What would you do differently if you could repeat the final phase of your leadership in a previous setting?
2. Do you feel that your predecessor prepared well for your leadership? If not, what might s/he have done differently to prepare the way for you? In turn, how are you helping the organization prepare for the day when you will no longer be there?
3. Make a list of things a "landing" leader can do to make his/her successor's "takeoff" go more smoothly.
4. Consider these passages from Scripture—Numbers 27:12-23; 2 Kings 2:1-18; John 13:1-20. How do the leaders prepare their successors in these texts? What strikes you about the transition, or transfer, of power?

Afterword

After a few lessons, with a nagging instructor always demanding higher levels of precision and perfection, student pilots begin setting their sights on the first solo. Earlier in the book, I told the story of my own solo flight more than thirty-five years ago. But as implied in the title of the book, my conviction is that as faithful people committed to exercise leadership through our God-given vocations, we are never alone. As people of faith, we are drawn prayerfully toward the destination, toward a future the Bible often describes as the "reign of God." Along the way there will be many surprises, unanticipated course corrections, diversions, and sometimes even surprising landing spots where we will sojourn for a season in a place not even imagined at the outset.

We are never in control

Unlike good pilots, however, faithful leaders are never really in control—of our own lives, our organizations, or the larger world in which we live and move and have our being. We pre-flight and plan, scan the environment in which we serve, contemplate the what ifs, seek to shed those things that cause us to stall, work in teams, try to avoid fixation on minor matters, evaluate our progress, and strive for happy landings. Nevertheless, in the end, leadership is gift and grace, not skill or human prowess. God is ultimately in control, the wind of the Spirit that holds us up when our wings may be clipped or damaged. Even if our wings should be taken from us altogether, the prayers will take us home!

In the meantime, however, we are called to move confidently, and boldly to point others toward the ultimate destination. So much of the time, in what's been described as the "postmodern" world, we are flying blind amidst turbulent, stormy conditions. The formerly well-established visual reference points that guided previous generations of faithful people are obscured and even obliterated altogether. Values and commitments that could be assumed in earlier times no longer hold sway for most people.

Pilots who lose sight of visual reference points and a dependable horizon are soon overcome with spatial disorientation or "vertigo." The loss of visual contact with the ground quickly allows the inner ear and brain to play tricks on the unsuspecting flier. Soon the airplane goes into a turn and begins either climbing or diving. The more the pilot tries to restore normal flight by "seat of the pants" sensations, the quicker things deteriorate, until finally the aircraft stalls and winds up in an unrecoverable spin. Death comes quickly, but the final moments must be terrifying.

Trust God's guiding gyroscope

For a pilot caught in a swirling, disorienting mass of clouds or an impenetrable fog bank, there is only one saving course of action: Trust the gyroscopes! These super-spinning mechanisms driven by electric power or a vacuum pump constitute the innards of the critical flight instruments. As long as a pilot believes her/his instruments and follows their indications, the airplane will be maintained in a safe and steady flight condition. But it is so hard to trust the instruments when all one's inner sensations are sending a different message.

Amidst all the swirling messages that bombard us on a daily basis, surrounded as we are with a cacophony of conflicting and unharmonious melodies and messages, our way forward as faithful leaders is to be found in trusting God's ever-dependable gyroscopes, pointing the way toward justice and *shalom*. Faithful, moral leadership hinges on attempting always to do the right thing, to be stewards holding ourselves accountable to the present and the future.

Bibliography

Badaracco, Joseph L., *Defining Moments: When Managers Must Choose between Right and Right.* Boston: Harvard Business School Press, 1996.

Becker, Carol E., *Becoming Colleagues: Women and Men Serving Together in Faith.* San Francisco: Jossey-Bass, 2000.

Bolman, Lee G. and Deal, Terrence E. 1997. *Reframing Organizations: Artistry, Choice, and Leadership.* San Francisco: Jossey-Bass.

Coles, Robert, *Lives of Moral Leadership.* 2000. New York: Random House.

Congregational Leader Series. 2002/3. Ten titles on various subjects, including strategic planning, conflict resolution, identifying and building staff, and mutual ministry. Minneapolis: Augsburg Fortress (see www.augsburgfortress.org/CLS).

Cooper, Robert K. and Sawaf, Ayman. 1996. *Executive EQ: Emotional Intelligence in Leadership and Organizations.* New York: The Berkley Publishing Group.

De Bono, Edward. 1999. *Six Thinking Hats.* Boston: Little, Brown and Company.

Friedman, Edwin. 1985. *Generation to Generation: Family Process in Church and Synagogue.* New York: The Guildford Press.

Gladwell, Malcolm. 2000. *The Tipping Point: How Little Things Can Make a Big Difference.* Boston: Little, Brown and Company.

Greenleaf, Robert K. 1991. *Servant Leadership.* New York: Paulist Press.

Hackman, J. Richard. 2002. *Leading Teams: Setting the Stage for Great Performances.* Boston: Harvard Business School Press.

Hagberg, Janet O. 1984. *Real Power: Stages of Personal Power in Organizations.* Minneapolis: Winston Press.

Hahn, Celia Allison. 1994. *Growing in Authority, Relinquishing Control.* Bethesda, MD: Alban Institute.

Heifetz, Ronald A. 1994. *Leadership Without Easy Answers.* Cambridge: Harvard Press.

Heifetz, Ronald A. and Linsky, Marty. 2002. *Leadership on the Line.* Boston: Harvard Business School Press.

Richardson, Ronald W. 1996. *Creating a Healthier Church: Family Systems Theory, Leadership, and Congregational Life.* Minneapolis: Fortress Press.

Senske, Kurt. 2003. *Executive Values: A Christian Approach to Organizational Leadership.* Minneapolis: Augsburg Books.

Turner, Nathan W. 1996. *Leading Small Groups: Basic Skills for Church and Community Organizations.* Valley Forge: Judson Press Series.

CONGREGATIONAL
LEADER SERIES
*Practical resources for congregational
planning and leadership development*

Congregational Planning
OUR CONTEXT
Exploring Our Congregation and Community
ISBN 0-8066-4404-4

OUR MISSION
Discovering God's Call to Us
ISBN 0-8066-4405-2

OUR STEWARDSHIP
Managing Our Assets
ISBN 0-8066-4406-0

OUR STRUCTURE
Carrying Out the Vision
ISBN 0-8066-4407-9

Leadership Development
CALLED TO LEAD
A Handbook for Lay Leaders
ISBN 0-8066-4412-5

GROWING TOGETHER, Rev. Ed.
Spiritual Exercises for Church Committees
ISBN 0-8066-4574-1

OUR COMMUNITY
Dealing with Conflict in Our Congregation
ISBN 0-8066-4411-7

OUR GIFTS
Identifying and Developing Leaders
ISBN 0-8066-4409-5

OUR STAFF
Building Our Human Resources
ISBN 0-8066-4410-9

PASTOR AND PEOPLE
Making Mutual Ministry Work
ISBN 0-8066-4651-9